FRAGMENT OF A PTOLEMAIC ROYAL ORDINANCE REGARDING THE TAX AND FEES TO BE COLLECTED
UPON SALES OF SLAVES

Columbia Papyrus Inventory Number 480, Reproduced in the Original Size

UPON SLAVERY IN PTOLEMAIC EGYPT

UPON SLAVERY
IN PTOLEMAIC EGYPT

WILLIAM LINN WESTERMANN

New York
COLUMBIA UNIVERSITY PRESS
1929

PRINTED IN THE UNITED STATES OF AMERICA
THE CAYUGA PRESS, ITHACA, NEW YORK

TO
AVRINA DAVIES WESTERMANN

UPON SLAVERY IN PTOLEMAIC EGYPT

The papyrus fragment which is here transcribed came to the library of Columbia University in a group of documents purchased in Egypt in December, 1926. The writing is with the fibres. The scribe shows a distinct tendency to accentuate the top of each line, by the length of the top stroke of his *taus* and *gammas*, by ligature of *eta* with following *iota*, of *gamma* with following *omicron* and *rho*, of *tau* with following *omicron* and *rho* (not consistently carried through) and sometimes with *epsilon* (line 20) and *omega* (line 3). This tendency is carried further by the straightness of the middle stroke of his *eta*. This characteristic, though quite as marked as in P. Halensis 1, is not carried to the degree which is to be found in B.G.U. VI 1297.[1] The upper line is broken by carrying above it the tops of the *alphas*, *deltas*, and *lambdas*. The final stroke of *nu* does not project above the upper line as in so many of the documents of the Zenon Archive. Certain of the letters, particularly the *tau* and *eta*, show a resemblance to those of B.G.U. III 1011,[2] of the early second century B.C., though in general the hand of P. Columbia 480 is finer than that of the Berlin papyrus.

Mr. H. Idris Bell, in the rapid conjectural dating on evidence of the script which he gave to this fragment in the process of distribution, placed it as of the late third century B.C. The appearance of the name of Dicaearchus in lines 7 and 21 fixes the date shortly before 197 B.C. This Dicaearchus, who had received a one per cent fee upon all slave sales between private persons (paragraphs 1-3) and was receiving, at the time the document was written, one drachma per head on those sold by forced public auction (paragraphs 4-5) as his grant (*dorea*) from the king, was obviously a personage of importance in Egypt.[3] The combination of the general dating by the script as about 200 B.C., the rare occurrence of the name Dicaearchus

---

[1] See the examples presented by W. Schubart in his *Palaeographie*, Munich, 1925, Abb. 3-6.

[2] To be seen in reproduction, in part, by Wilhelm Schubart, *Papyri Graecae Berolinenses*, Bonn, 1911, 7a.

[3] There is the possibility that the πρότερον of πρότερον λογευομένηι εἰς τὴν Δικαιάρχου δωρεάν of lines 6-7 is to be understood throughout the document where the grant of Dicaearchus is mentioned. In that case the account into which was paid the one drachma fee upon slaves sold at public auction, recorded in lines 17-18 and line 22, must have retained, on the finance records, its designation as "the *dorea* of Dicaearchus" after the fee itself [*Continued on page 2*

1

in the papyri, and the fact that the only Dicaearchus of importance who has as yet appeared in the annals of Ptolemaic Egypt was the Aetolian of that name, the piratical mercenary who served in the army of Ptolemy V under the Aetolian general Scopas, gives the date of the document as about 198-197 B.C.[4]

The fragment consists of one column broken at the bottom and six or seven letters at the beginning of the first four lines of a second column. Two methods were employed by the copyist in marking the divisions of the document: (1) by the projection of one letter at the beginning of each new paragraph; and (2) by the use of *paragraphai*, which are preserved after sections 1, 2, 4 and 5, and are presumably to be supplied in the lacunae after the other paragraphs.

There is no indication that other columns preceded col. I. The fragmentary beginning of col. II indicates that the general subject of the sale of slaves was continued in that column, though perhaps not the specific subject of col. I, which deals with the amount of the tax and fees upon sales of slaves. A small piece, about a quarter of an inch in depth, projecting below the middle of col. I, line 28, shows no letters. The suggested restoration of line 29, of which this small piece would be a part, is not long enough to extend over it. It is impossible, therefore, to determine the original depth of the columns. Col. I deals, in the first three paragraphs (lines 1-15), with the taxes on ordinary commercial transfers of slaves, and in the last four paragraphs (lines 15-29) with the sales which occurred through judicial decision, through arrears to the fiscal department, and through enslavement for debt. Whether the taxes collected upon manumissions may be the subject of the first paragraph of col. II, or whether they may have appeared on a lower part of col. I, I can not determine.

had reverted to the state. For this possibility see the discussion of the taxes paid into "the *dorea* of Agathocles," p. 29, note 65c. Assuming that the πρότερον is to be understood wherever the *dorea* of Dicaearchus is mentioned, the *diagramma* would have to be dated *after* 197 B.C. But I cannot accept the idea of an omission so important as that of πρότερον would have been in a matter vital to the fiscus. Accepting the text, therefore, as it stands, I conclude that the clerical tax of lines 17-18 and line 22 was still being paid to Dicaearchus as his *dorea* when the *diagramma* was written, and I date the royal ordinance in 197 B.C. or in the year just preceding.

[4] The problem of the chronology will be discussed more fully later. For Dicaearchus see Diodorus Siculus XXVIII 1, Polybius XVIII 54-55, and cf. Maurice Holleaux in *Revue des Études*

Fayum   7 1/4 x 5 1/4 in.   c. 198-197 B.C.

Col. I

ἐκ τοῦ διαγράμματος τοῦ τ[ῶ]ν ἀνδραπό[δ]ω[ν.

ὁ πραγματευόμενος τὴν ὠνὴν τῶν ἀνδραπόδων

καὶ ὁ ἀντιγραφεὺς πράξονται τῶν σωμάτων

ὧν ἂν αἱ ὠναὶ ἐπὶ τῶν ἀγορανόμων καταγράφωνται

5   τῆς τιμῆς ἧς ἂν καταγράφωνται πρὸς ἀργύριον

παρὰ τοῦ ἀποδ[ο]μένου σὺν τῆι ἑ[κα]τοστῆ[ι] πρ[ό-

τερον λογευομένηι εἰς τὴν Δικαιάρχου δωρεὰν

τῆς μνᾶς (δραχμὰς) (ἐννέα) (διώβολον) (ἥμισυ) καὶ παρὰ τοῦ

        ἀ[γορ]άσαντος (δραχμὰς) (ὀκτώ) (διώβολον) [(ἥμισυ)

ὥστε γίνεσθαι τῆς μνᾶς (δραχμὰς) (ἑπτακαίδεκα) (πεντώβολον)

        [καὶ] τῆι πόλει προ-

10 πωλητικὸν παρὰ τοῦ ἀποδομέν[ο]υ τοῦ σώματο[ς] (δραχμὰς)

        (τέτταρας) (ὀβολόν).

ἐὰν δέ τις ἀγοράσηι ἐφ' ὧι τὰ τέλη πάντα καταβ[α]λεῖ

πράξονται τῆι μνᾶι (δραχμὰς) (εἴκοσι) (ὀβολόν) καὶ τῆι πόλ[ει]

        τοῦ σ[ώ]ματο[ς] (δραχμὰς) (τέτταρας) [(ὀβολόν).

ἐὰν δέ τις ἐξ ὑπερβολῆς ἢ ἀνθυπερβο[λῆ]ς κατάσχ[ηι

προσκαταβαλεῖ τῆι πόλει ἄλλο προπρατι[κ]όν.

15 τῶν] δὲ πωλουμένων διὰ ξενικῶν πράκτορ[ος

π]ράξο[ν]ται οἱ ἀγοράσαντες τῆς μ[νᾶς] (δραχμὰς) (ἐννεακαίδεκα)

        καὶ

κηρ[ύκειον ἑ]κατοστὴν (δραχμὴν) (μίαν) καὶ εἰς [τὴν] δωρεὰν

γραφῖ[ο]ν τοῦ σώματος (δραχμὴν) (μίαν).

τῶν δὲ πρὸς βασιλικὰ πωλουμένων π[ρα]χθήσοντα[ι] οἱ

20 ἀγοράσ[α]ντες τῆς μνᾶς (δραχμὰς) (ἐκκαίδεκα) (πεντώβολον)

        κα[ὶ κ]ηρύκειον ἑ-

3

κατοστὴν (δραχμὴν) (μίαν) καὶ γραφῖον εἰς τὴν Δικαιάρχ[ο]υ
δωρεὰν τοῦ σώματος (δραχμὴν) (μίαν).

τ]ῶν δὲ ὑποχρέων σωμάτων ὅσα ἂν ἐλεύ[θε]ρα ὄντα ἑαυ-
τὰ c.10 letters   ] τὸ χρέος πράξονται τὸν δα[ν]είζον-

25   τα τῆς μνᾶς] (δραχμὰς) (πέντε) (ὀβολὸν) καὶ τὸν δανειζόμε[νο]ν
                 (δραχμὰς) (πέντε) (ὀβολὸν)

     ὥστ' εἶναι τῆι] μνᾶι (δραχμὰς) (δέκα) (διώβολον) καὶ γραφῖον
           τοῦ σ[ώ]ματ[ο]ς (δραχμὴν) (μίαν).

c. 14 letters   ]αι πρὸς τὸ χρέος πρ[άξ]ονται τὸν[
        τῆς μνᾶς (δραχμὰς)] (πεντώβολον) κα[ὶ] ἐκατ[οσ]τὴν
        [(δραχμὴν) (μίαν) καὶ
γραφῖον τοῦ σώματος δραχμὴν μίαν. ?]

Col. II

30 ὁ] δ' ἀναπ[ἧι ἂν ἡμέραι ἀπο-
    γράψητ[αι
    αὐθήμερο[ν

      ]..ια.[

Col. I

1. Only a slight trace of the ε remains. Cf. ἐκ τοῦ πολιτικοῦ νόμου
in P. Halensis 1.79, and ἐκ τοῦ ἐγκυκλίου in B.G.U. VI 1213, 7.

4. For the important reading, ἐπὶ τῶν ἀγορανόμων καταγράφωνται,
I am indebted to the well-known kindness and the papyrological knowledge
of Professor Ulrich Wilcken. His reading, made from a rough photostat
copy sent to him by me, is now completely confirmed by the original after
redamping and straightening of the fibres at this point.

8. The first number must be read either as ε or as θ. The two-obol sign
after it is clear on the original. The last number is certainly η as determined
by the perpendicular stroke on the left, appearing clearly on the shreds, and
the characteristic looped point at the right upper corner of the η. As the
total is given in the next line as 17 drachmas 5 obols, the addition of the half-

obol at the end of the line, reading $\eta = [c$, is necessary, though no trace of the half-obol sign appears on the papyrus surface. In the same way the π at the beginning of line 16 is lost without apparent breakage of the surface, and the ω of $\sigma[\acute{\omega}]\mu\alpha\tau o[s]$ in line 12.

14-15. There is no trace of a *paragraphos* between these two lines. Apparently it is lost in the breaking off of upper fibres at this point.

16. Read $\pi\rho\alpha\chi\theta\acute{\eta}\sigma o\nu\tau\alpha\iota$, as in line 19, although $\pi]\rho\acute{\alpha}\xi o[\nu]\tau\alpha\iota$ seems to me to be the actual reading of the original according to the available space and the traces of the letters which remain. In regarding $\pi]\rho\acute{\alpha}\xi o[\nu]\tau\alpha\iota$ here as a copyist's error for $\pi\rho\alpha\chi\theta\acute{\eta}\sigma o\nu\tau\alpha\iota$ I have adopted a suggestion of Ulrich Wilcken, which has cleared up many difficulties arising out of the attempt to retain the future middle form.

20. Parts of the two horizontal bars of the five-obol sign are visible along the edges of a small hole at this point.

21. There is a pen-stroke under the second letter, *alpha*, which resembles a large *omicron*, open at the top. I cannot bring it into any relation with the text. It is not a *koronis*.

24. The sense seems to demand $\acute{\epsilon}\alpha\upsilon[\tau\grave{\alpha} \pi\rho o\sigma\delta\hat{\omega}\iota \pi\rho\grave{o}s] \tau\grave{o} \chi\rho\acute{\epsilon}os$ or $\acute{\epsilon}\alpha\upsilon[\tau\grave{\alpha} \acute{\upsilon}\pi o\theta\hat{\eta}\iota \epsilon\grave{\iota}s] \tau\grave{o} \chi\rho\acute{\epsilon}os$, with the preference for the former restoration. The use of $\acute{\upsilon}\pi o\tau\iota\theta\acute{\epsilon}\nu\alpha\iota$ with the person is rare. Cf. for the Zenon period P.S.I. IV 424, 13, and for the Byzantine period P. Meyer, *Juristische Papyri*, 12, 15, $\acute{\upsilon}\pi o\tau\epsilon\theta\epsilon\iota\kappa[\acute{o}\tau os] \tau\acute{o}\tau\epsilon \tau\grave{\eta}\nu . . . \acute{\alpha}\delta\epsilon\lambda\varphi\acute{\eta}\nu$.

25. One must allow here in the lacuna for the customary blank space before the drachma sign.

26. The space does not permit $[\acute{\omega}\sigma\tau\epsilon \gamma\acute{\iota}\nu\epsilon\sigma\theta\alpha\iota]$.

27. Only the tops of the first two letters following the lacuna appear. The first letter must be either α, δ or λ. $\pi\rho\grave{o}s \tau\grave{o} \chi\rho\acute{\epsilon}os$, which I have repeatedly read under different lighting, seems to me to be fairly certain. The remaining traces of the letters are slight, however. The space precludes the reading $\pi\rho\grave{o}s \beta\alpha\sigma\iota\lambda\iota\kappa\acute{\alpha}$.

28. Either $\tau\grave{o}\nu [\acute{\alpha}\gamma o\rho\acute{\alpha}\sigma\alpha\nu\tau\alpha \tau\hat{\eta}s \mu\nu\hat{\alpha}s]$ or $\tau\grave{o}\nu [\delta\alpha\nu\epsilon\acute{\iota}\zeta o\nu\tau\alpha \tau\hat{\eta}s \mu\nu\hat{\alpha}s]$ seems to be required.

Col. II

30. $\acute{o}] \delta' \acute{\alpha}\nu\alpha\pi$ [, because of the singular, $\gamma\rho\acute{\alpha}\psi\eta\tau[\alpha\iota$, in the following line.

TRANSLATION

From the royal ordinance upon the slaves.

The contractor of the tax on the slaves and the antigrapheus shall collect upon the slaves whose sales may be recorded before the *agoranomi*, upon the price at which they may be recorded, in silver [as follows]: from the seller, including the one per cent tax formerly collected for the *dorea* of Dicaearchus, per mina, 9 drachmas 2 1/2 obols; and from the buyer 8 drachmas 2 1/2 obols; total per mina, 17 drachmas 5 obols; and for the city as brokerage fee from the seller, per head, 4 drachmas 1 obol.

If anyone buys [a slave] on the basis that he will pay all the taxes, they [the tax farmers] shall collect, per mina, 20 drachmas 1 obol and for the city, per head, 4 drachmas 1 obol.

If anyone gains possession of a slave in consequence of a higher bid or a counterbid, he shall pay to the city another brokerage fee.

Upon those sold through the *praktores xenikon* the purchasers shall pay, per mina, 19 drachmas, and as crier's fee a one per cent tax, 1 drachma, and for the *dorea* as clerical fee, per head, 1 drachma.

Upon those being sold in consequence of debts to the royal treasury the purchasers shall pay, per mina, 16 drachmas 5 obols, and as crier's fee a one per cent tax, 1 drachma, and as clerical fee for the *dorea* of Dicaearchus, per head, 1 drachma.

Upon persons enslaved for debt, as many as, when free, may have . . . the debt, they shall collect from the lender, per mina, 5 drachmas 1 obol, and from the borrower 5 drachmas 1 obol, total per mina 10 drachmas 2 obols, and as clerical fee, per head, 1 drachma.

. . . in relation to the debt, they shall collect [from the purchaser?] . . . drachmas 5 obols and as one per cent tax 1 drachma [and as clerical fee, per head, 1 drachma?].

The heading of col. I clearly indicates the source and character of the document. It is an extract (ἐκ τοῦ διαγράμματος) copied out of the *diagramma* (royal ordinance) upon the slaves. The complete ordinance must have covered numerous phases of the slave trade in its relation to the fiscal department of the Ptolemaic state. The particular section which is here preserved was presumably copied, along with other materials, for use or for reference in the Fayum, where it was found. This portion of the complete *diagramma* deals solely with the sales of slaves and the relations between the farmers of the slave sale tax and the tax payers. It is directed to the tax farmers (see lines 2-3, ὁ πραγματευόμενος τὴν ὠνὴν τῶν ἀνδραπόδων καὶ ὁ ἀντιγραφεὺς πράξονται). More particularly, col. I deals in the main with only two essential points: (1) the amount of the tax and the fees, and (2) the incidence of these taxes as between seller and buyer or the parties corresponding to them, including the variations, both in amount and incidence, under different conditions of sale.[5] Other conclusions may be drawn, as to the leasing of the farming privilege for the tax on slave sales and as to the officials connected with it; but these are incidental to the actual subject of this extract.

It is evident throughout the document that it deals with the taxes on *transfers of slaves, not on the ownership of them.*[6] In the first three sections the sales are voluntary transfers, regular commercial transactions, between individual buyers and sellers of slaves. The remaining paragraphs of col. I determine the taxes and fees to be collected in cases of compulsory sales resulting from court decisions, arrears to the government, or personal execution upon a debtor. Throughout the document ὁ πραγματευόμενος τὴν ὠνὴν[7] καὶ ὁ ἀντιγραφεὺς of lines 2-3 are to be understood as the collectors of the taxes (τὰ τέλη, l. 11). These are the official terms, respectively, for the tax contractor and for the clerk of the oeconomus who provided the government's check upon the activities and the collections of the *pragmateuomenos.* Both are well known from the Revenue Laws of Philadelphus. In section 4, as the *diagramma* states (lines 15-18), the sales are *managed* by the ξενικῶν πράκτορες in the case of court judgments; and the assumption is that, in the cases of sales which occurred through arrears to the fiscal department (section 5, lines 19-22), the auctions would be conducted by

[5] Paragraphs 2 and 3 do not definitely state from whom the collectors are to exact the tax and fees; but in both cases it is clear from the context that the purchaser is to pay them.

[6] Lines 3-4, πράξονται τῶν σωμάτων, ὧν ἂν αἱ ὠναί; line 6, παρὰ τοῦ ἀποδομένου; line 15. τῶν δὲ πωλουμένων διὰ ξενικῶν πράκτορος. For an example of the sales tax on slave transfers of the year 143 A.D. see P. Freib. 8, 15: τεταγμένην ὑπὲρ αὐτῶν τῇ τῶν ἀνδραπόδων ὠνῇ τὸ καθῆκον τέλος (*Sitz. Heid. Akad., ph.-hist. Kl. VII,* 10 Abh.), and thereto Partsch, *ibid.* p. 26. Cf. B.G.U. 1059, 9; P. Lips. 445 (=Mitteis, *Papyruskunde, Chrest.* 171, 30 f.).

[7] For the meaning of ὠνή as the tax farming privilege see M. Rostovtzeff, "Geschichte der Staatspacht in der rönischen Kaiserzeit," German revision in *Philologus,* Suppl., IX 333; U. Wilcken, *Griechische Ostraka* p. 531.

officials of that bureau. Accepting Wilcken's suggestion, that π]ράξονται of line 16 is an error in copying for πραχθήσονται, ὁ ἀγοράσας and οἱ ἀγοράσαντες consistently refer to the purchasers of slaves throughout.[8]

As to the meanings of the two words σῶμα and ἀνδράποδον, both used in this document for "slave," σῶμα as it appears in the papyri may or may not, if otherwise undefined, mean "slave."[9] Ordinarily, when standing alone, it conveys no implication as to the legal status of the person concerned[10] and is to be translated as "person" or "workman." In P. Col. Inv. 480 the genitive form, τοῦ σώματος, displays this colorless use (frequently met in accounts) in lines 10, 12, 18, 22, 26; and I have correspondingly translated it "per head" in these places. When the context makes its meaning quite clear, as frequently in wills, σῶμα may stand alone for "slave" (see P. Petrie III 11, line 20). Such is its significance in our document in line 3 (πράξονται τῶν σωμάτων). Even in wills of the period of the Roman Empire further definition seems to be customary, as in δοῦλα σώματα of P. Oxy. 492, 7 and 12, and of P. Freib. 8, 14. The usage of σώματα with defining adjective for "slaves" is apparent in the combination τῶν ὑποχρέων σωμάτων of line 23 of P. Col. Inv. 480; for I take it to be certain, from their inclusion in the royal ordinance on the slaves (τὸ τῶν ἀνδραπόδων διάγραμμα), from the statement that they were once free (ὅσα ἂν ἐλεύθερα ὄντα), and from the combination with σώματα (which would otherwise have no meaning), that these debtors (ὑπόχρεοι), for fiscal purposes and in the eyes of the finance department, were regarded as slaves. ἀνδράποδον in this document is used as a *general* word for "slave" and does not seem to differ from δοῦλος.[11]

The distinction made above, that sections 1-3 treat of voluntary sales and sections 4-7 of compulsory transfers, involving action of the court officials

---

[8] In the Revenue Papyrus ὁ ἀγοράσας is used to designate the tax farmer only with τὴν ὠνήν (34, 11; 42, 2; cf. P. Paris 62, col. I, in U.P.Z. 112), or where the reference to the tax farmer is clear (ὁ τὴν Σαΐτην ἀγοράσας, 66, 23 et passim).

[9] See Vitelli in the introduction to P.S.I. 423.

[10] As in Wilcken, *Chrestomathie* 198, of 240 B.C., in which a Fayum dweller lists himself, his four sons, a nurse, and eight farmers as σώ(ματα) ιε, that is, "fifteen persons." Of these the nurse and some of the farmers may, or may not, be slaves. Cf. the farm hands called σώματα in the Zenon papyrus, P. Cairo Zenon III 59517.

[11] See the use of οἰκέται δοῦλοι and ἀνδράποδα in P. Lille 29. The interpretation of the editors of P. Hibeh 29, that ἀνδράποδα in that document meant prisoners of war, certainly cannot be applied to its use in P. Col. Inv. 480. Cf. G. Plaumann in *Sitz. Heid. Akad.*, 1914, *ph.-hist. Kl.* 14, p. 10, note 2.

or other government agencies, is to be accepted only with the following warning. The entire process of slave sales was under complete government control, both the voluntary sales of sections 1-3 and the compulsory sales. This is made clear by the fact that, even in the case of these voluntary sales, a brokerage fee (*propoletikon* in lines 9-10, *propratikon* in line 14)[12] was collected by the government and paid "to the city" (*i.e.*, Alexandria). The state, therefore, regarded itself as handling all the slave sales, and collected a fee as middleman even where all arrangements had previously been made by the parties to the sale, as is the case in paragraph 1. In the compulsory sales of paragraphs 4-7 the government was a party in each transaction. Its own officials handled the sales in such cases in the government's interest. Therefore no broker's fee was exacted.

INTERPRETATION BY PARAGRAPHS
Paragraph 1, lines 1-10

"The contractor of the tax on the slaves and the antigrapheus shall collect upon the slaves whose sales may be recorded before the *agoranomi* [notaries and market supervisors], upon the price at which they may be recorded, in silver [as follows]: from the seller, including the one per cent tax formerly collected for the *dorea* of Dicaearchus, per mina, 9 drachmas 2 1/2 obols; and from the buyer 8 drachmas 2 1/2 obols; total per mina, 17 drachmas 5 obols; and for the city as brokerage fee from the seller, per head, 4 drachmas 1 obol."

The prime importance of this paragraph lies in the appearance and interpretation of the καταγραφή, the official recording of a sale, expressed in the καταγράφωνται of lines 4 and 5. This appearance of the καταγραφή is the second earliest instance of the use of the term in an incontestible reading, following that in B.G.U. VI 1213, of the third century B.C. It seems best, therefore, in view of the extensive discussion of the καταγραφή and the differences of opinion regarding it, first to establish its use and significance from the present document.

Paragraph 1 deals with the amount of taxes and fees to be collected by the tax farmers, and the distribution of these between seller and buyer, on a certain type of sale between the slave owner and a prospective buyer, without

[12] Cf. the arrangement for middleman's fee in the sale of oil in Alexandria in P. Rev. 55, 15.

preliminary aid or intervention by any government agency. In sales of this type the agreements reached between the two interested parties are presented at the offices of the *agoranomi* and registered officially in their presence (ὧν ἂν αἱ ὠναὶ ἐπὶ τῶν ἀγορανόμων καταγράφωνται, l. 4). αἱ ὠναὶ here means "the sales" in general, rather than specifically "the documents of sale,"[13] as is shown by the following line (l. 5, τῆς τιμῆς ἧς ἂν καταγράφωνται), "at the price at which they [*i.e.*, the sales] may be recorded." The correct reading of line 5, gained by Ulrich Wilcken, gives splendid confirmation of his reading of the Ptolemaic document, P. Lond. II 220, p. 5, l. 11, a complaint of 133 B.C.: οὐχ ὑ]πομένει τὴν κατα[γραφὴν μοι] ποιήσασθαι ἐπ' ἀ[γορανό]μου.[14] Although that document is very fragmentary, it seems to deal with the sale of a house,[15] in which the purchaser complains that the vendor had not carried out the act of official recording. P. Col. Inv. 480 confirms the conclusion drawn by Schönbauer from P. Lond. 220 that the activity of the *agoranomus* was regarded as accessory to that of the vendor, who, according to P. Lond. 220 and P. Col. Inv. 480 as well, seems to be responsible for the *katagraphe*[16] (ἐπὶ τοῦ ἀγορανόμου, in both places).

From paragraph 1 of the Columbia *diagramma* two conclusions may be drawn as to the official recording of sales of slaves:[17]

(1) The document of record presented at the office of the market supervisor (*agoranomus*) contained a statement of the price agreed upon between vendor and purchaser.

(2) The taxes on slave sales were collected as a percentage of the sale price contained in this document of record. The tax farmers, therefore, in

---

[13] ὠνή sometimes has the meaning "deed of sale." See the deed of sale of a slave girl, Sphragis, from Nicanor to Zenon, of 259 B.C. (P. Cairo Zenon 59003), designated on the verso as ὠνὴ παιδίσκη[ς; P. Lond. III 1206, 2 (p. 15), ὠνὴ Πανοβχου( ) . . . γῆς; and compare the suggested translation of τὰς ὠνάς of P. Hal. 1, 246 in *Dikaiomata*, p. 249.

[14] See Ernst Schönbauer, *Beiträge zur Geschichte des Liegenschaftsrechtes im Altertum*, Leipzig, 1924, p. 27. The reading given above differs slightly from that presented by Schönbauer, in accordance with the citation from his own copy which Wilcken sent to me by letter.

[15] Schönbauer, p. 27.

[16] See Schönbauer, p. 28. For the activity of the offices of the *agoranomi* in receiving the *declarations* (ἀπογραφαί) of slaves mortgaged for a debt, see P. Hibeh 29 (of about 265 B.C. = Wilcken *Chrestomathie*, 259) and cf. Schönbauer, p. 30.

[17] For the classification of slaves in Greek law as immobile property see Schönbauer, *Liegenschaftsrecht*, p. 18. The handling of real property sales should, therefore, parallel closely the handling of slave sales.

the case of such a sale arranged between the parties interested in the trans-action, exacted the tax and fees concurrently with the filing of the official record at the office of the *agoranomus*. The deed of sale (ὠνή) must have been in completed form, with price agreed upon.

A third conclusion depends upon the observation that the type of sale treated in paragraph 1 is the only kind of sale appearing in our document in which the *katagraphe* was employed. The sales of paragraphs 4-7 were con-ducted by state machinery in which the official recording was automatically cared for. The sale with *katagraphe* before the market supervisors, in para-graph 1, was likewise distinguished from those of paragraphs 2 and 3, although these also were sales between private persons which were in no way due to legal compulsion. In paragraph 3 this distinction becomes apparent as one based upon the fact that the government auctioning agency conducts the sales envisaged in that paragraph. Through this fact the government record, with sale price, was again automatically provided for, by the process of public auction. Paragraph 2, which is to be interpreted in connection with paragraph 3, also refers to sale by auction and is without the requirement of *katagraphe*. The third conclusion, therefore, is the obvious one that the recording of sales of slaves before the *agoranomi* was not required where official record was cared for by the activity of the government agencies. We may accept as established the fact of the official recording, before the *agora-nomi*, of private sales of slaves in Ptolemaic Egypt at about 200 B.C. (P. Col. Inv. 480) and in 133 B.C. (P. Lond. II 220, p. 5). The document for record was presented by the vendor. The *katagraphe* was the official act of the *agora-nomus*. The recording document contained the sale price. On the basis of these facts the mooted question of the form and legal significance of the *katagraphe* must be approached.[18] In the matter of sales of *immobilia*, in-cluding slaves, the prospective vendor must first make a *declaration*, by *apographe*, of his intention to sell. P. Hibeh 29 (= Wilcken, *Chrest.* 259),

[18] The literature upon the *katagraphe* problem is extensive. The references to the primary sources will be found in convenient form in A. Schwarz, "Die öffentliche und private Urkunde in römischen Aegypten" (*Abh. Sächs. Akad., ph.-hist. Kl.*, XXXI no. 3), Leipzig, 1920, p. 227, note 1, followed by citation of the secondary literature, up to 1920, in note 4 to pp. 228-229. To these Schönbauer's discussion in his *Liegenschaftsrecht*, Leipzig, 1924, and Egon Weiss, *Greichisches Privatrecht*, Leipzig, 1928, p. 215, are to be added. Cf. also P. M. Meyer in *Sav.-Ztsch.* XLVI p. 309.

dated at about 265 B.C., has to do with the sales of mortgaged slaves (see ὁ ὑποτεθείς, l. 6)[19] and with the protection of the interests of the farmer of the sale tax. From that document it is apparent that prospective sales must be declared beforehand, *and through the offices of the market supervisors* (the *agoranomi*, ἢ μὴ ἀπογράψητα[ι διὰ τῶν] ἀγορανομίων, ll. 2-3). Lists[20] of the slave sales were to be made out by the joint activity of the "clerk of the slaves," the checking clerk and the tax farmer; and the tax farmer was obligated to copy this document upon a notice board and set up the notice board before the office of the *agoranomus*. In P. Gradenwitz 1,[21] which clearly stands in some close relationship to the subject of P. Col. Inv. 480, the requirement appears that all persons who are interested in the purchase of the slaves which are the subject of that document must declare themselves at Alexandria (l. 7, ἀπογραψ[άσ]θω[σαν, Wilcken's reading). For that particular case, definite time limits have been specified for the declarations.[22] One must assume that similar declarations (ἀπογραφαί) of intention to sell slaves, or otherwise transfer them, were required for all transfers in the Ptolemaic period, including those of P. Col. Inv. 480, in the interest of the government control of the slave-selling privilege.

The *katagraphe* problem of the Ptolemaic period in Schönbauer's discussion revolves largely about the restoration of P. Halensis I, XI,[23] which deals with the sale of houses and building lots in the city of Alexandria. Schönbauer's restoration of the beginning of XI § 2 ([οἱ δὲ ταμίαι καταγρα]φόντωσαν τὰς ὠνάς in place of the ἀναγρα]φόντωσαν τὰς ὠνάς of the editors), which was already strongly supported by B.G.U. VI 1213,[24] receives further support from the use of the verb καταγράφειν in the Columbia document. The

---

[19] Cf. Schönbauer, *Liegenschaftsrecht*, p. 30.

[20] The type of sale envisaged in P. Hibeh 29 seems to be that of mortgaged slaves. See ὁ ὑπ[οτε]θείς in line 6 and τὰς ὑποθέσεις, probably equivalent to τὰς ὑποθήκας, in line 7.

[21] First published by Gerhard Plaumann in *Sitz. Heid. Akad., phil.-hist. Kl.*, V (1914), Abh. 15, with comments by Ulrich Wilcken from a letter to Plaumann. The document was later republished by H. Lewald, with the addition of a fragment found in the Frankfurt collection, in *Raccolta Lumbroso*.

[22] See Lewald's transcription, *op. cit.*, p. 340, lines 7-12.

[23] *Dikaiomata*, Berlin, 1913, pp. 140 ff.

[24] A list of citations of laws, with brief statement of their contents, of the third century B.C. The reference to the *katagraphe* (lines 9-10) is a citation of "royal decrees that the treasurers shall not record sales (ὠνὰς μὴ καταγράφειν τοὺς ταμίας) unless he [the seller] has shown how he came into possession."

question of the precise form of the *katagraphe* and of its legal significance is one for the competent juristic scholars to decide. To the discussion of the legal intent and result of the *katagraphe*, its appearance in the Columbia document brings one definite contribution. It is not the acquirer of the property who is here the subject of the passive form καταγράφεσθαι; but it is the "sales" which are recorded.[25] The explanation of Schönbauer was that in its Ptolemaic use the *katagraphe* was the official act of recording sales which brought to its legal completion the business transacted by the parties concerned.[26] Schönbauer's argument, on its grammatical side, receives complete support from the Columbia document as against that of Josef Partsch, who made the acquirer of the property the object of καταγράφειν (in the sense that the seller, by documentary declaration, recognized him as the new owner) and subject of the passive καταγράφεσθαι because he had been recognized as new owner by the former owner.[27] The portion of the *diagramma* on the slaves which is preserved in the Columbia fragment contains instructions to the tax farmers upon the sale tax on slaves. Its information upon the *katagraphe*, therefore, is confined to that aspect of the taxation on slaves in which the tax collectors were interested, namely, the price paid. Upon this sale price their percentage for collection was to be based. The Columbia document, therefore, emphasizes the fiscal importance of the records of sales in the offices of the *agoranomi* more strongly than has heretofore been done in the legal discussions upon the *katagraphe*.

The actual state tax collected on the slaves sold under the system explained in paragraph 1 was 16 drachmas 5 obols upon the mina, with the addition of a fee of 1 drachma to the mina (the ἑκατοστή of line 6), making the total of 17 drachmas 5 obols of line 9. The *hekatoste* (one per cent fee) which occurs in this paragraph (line 6) and is to be assumed in paragraphs 2-3, differs in amount from the *graphion* (clerical fee) recorded in paragraphs 4-5 as still going to the grant to Dicaearchus.[28] The income from the one per

---

[25] P. Col. Inv. 480, 5: τῆς τιμῆς ῆς ἅν καταγράφωνται (*scil.* αἱ ὠναί, to which the meaning of "sales documents" cannot here be applied).

[26] *Liegenschaftsrecht*, p. 26.

[27] See Josef Partsch in the introduction to P. Freiburg 8, in *Sitz. Heid. Akad.* VII (1916), Abh. 10, p. 14.

[28] The fee, under the system of leases discussed in paragraph 1, is applied at one per cent *ad valorem*. The γραφῖον of paragraphs 4-5 is a specific duty of 1 drachma per slave sold.

cent fee, which I identify with the κηρύκειον ἑκατοστήν of lines 17 and 20-21, had once been allocated to the *dorea* of Dicaearchus, but had now reverted to the government, the clerical fee of sections 4-5 (possibly also of sections 6-7) taking its place as his *dorea*. To the total tax collected for the uses of the central government, which amounted to 17 5/6 per cent of the sale price, there was added a brokerage fee of 4 drachmas 1 obol which was levied for 'the city" ([καὶ] τῆι πόλει προπωλητικόν, lines 9-10). This fee was assessed *per slave sold*, not per mina. The "city" here referred to must be Alexandria.

The exaction of the tax was as follows: The seller of the slave paid 9 drachmas 2 1/2 obols per mina of the tax, plus the brokerage fee of 4 drachmas 1 obol (per slave sold) to the city. The purchaser was responsible for the remaining 8 drachmas 2 1/2 obols per mina of the total tax of 17 drachmas 5 obols per mina. It is important to note that *the tax was assessed upon the value of the slave sold*,[29] except for the item of the brokerage fee to the city. Notable, also, is the high percentage of the tax.

Paragraph 2, lines 11-12

"If anyone buys [a slave] on the basis that he will pay all the taxes, they [the tax farmers] shall collect, per mina, 20 drachmas 1 obol and for the city, per head, 4 drachmas 1 obol."

The interpretation of this section depends upon the observation that the official record (*katagraphe*) was not made before the market supervisors with respect to the sales with which the paragraph deals. The difficulty which it presents arises from the abbreviated form of the fragment of the complete *diagramma* represented by P. Col. Inv. 480 because it intends to convey only that information which would be useful to the tax farmers. Paragraphs 1-3 have been already distinguished as voluntary transfers of slaves, as contrasted with paragraphs 4-7, which are concerned with sales under some form of official compulsion. Paragraph 1 determines the tax rate upon *all* sales which are recorded before the market supervisors, the tax being divided between buyer and seller. Paragraphs 2 and 3 deal with sales which require no *katagraphe*. The official record in such sales must, therefore, occur auto-

[29] Gerhard Plaumann in his discussion of P. Gradenwitz 1, in *Sitz. Heid. Akad.* V (1914), Abh. 15, p. 11, considered that the tax on slaves of P. Grad. 1 (which he explains as a tax on the ownership of slaves) was assessed without reference to the value of the slave.

matically in the process of the sale. Paragraph 3 is concerned with slaves sold by auction; but it only refers to those auctions in which a second bidding, or a second and a third bidding, have occurred. Paragraph 2 must, in consequence, contain the instructions to the tax farmers on sales by auction in which the primary bidding has been decisive. This conclusion is necessary, because otherwise the tax farmers would be without instructions as to the amount and incidence of the slave sale tax on such sales. For them the subject of paragraph 2 was clear enough, for two reasons. The auction sale in voluntary transfers would be known to them as that type of sale between private persons in which the purchaser agreed to pay all the taxes; and they would interpret the paragraph in connection with paragraph 3, in which the instructions are given for sales at auction in which higher bids and counterbids might be received.

Under these conditions of sale, using the government's auctioning system for handling slaves declared for voluntary sale by private individuals, the purchaser pays all the tax. The indefinite $\tau\iota s$ certainly refers to the purchaser; and the subjects of $\pi\rho\acute{a}\xi o\nu\tau a\iota$ are the tax farmer and the *antigrapheus* of lines 2-3. Under this system of transfer the actual sale tax was 20 drachmas 1 obol per mina (which must have included the one per cent fee formerly allocated to Dicaearchus), as against the total of 17 drachmas 5 obols under the system of paragraph 1. The brokerage tax ($\pi\rho o\pi\omega\lambda\eta\tau\iota\kappa\acute{o}\nu$) paid to the city remained the same, at 4 drachmas 1 obol per slave. This also was to fall upon the purchaser, making the total of his obligations to the government 24 drachmas 2 obols per mina on each slave purchased. On a slave purchased at 300 drachmas[30] the *purchaser* would pay 64 drachmas 4 obols under system two as against 32 drachmas 2 1/2 obols under the system used in paragraph 1.

The advance in the actual sale tax (including the one per cent fee, but not including the *propoletikon*) under this sale by auction (20 1/6 per cent *ad valorem* as against 17 5/6 per cent *ad valorem* under the sale by agreement with *katagraphe*) would tend to equalize the income to the government with that which it would have obtained under the system of paragraph 1. If, for example, a slave were offered by his owner at 300 drachmas and sold at

[30] Fr. Oertel has estimated the price of slaves in the third century B.C. at about 330 drachmas. See Plaumann, *Sitz. Heid. Akad.* V 15, p. 17.

that price under the first system, the government tax plus the fees on the sale would have amounted to 57 drachmas 4 obols (at 17 5/6 per cent plus brokerage fee). If sold under the second system at 250 drachmas, the government would still have taken in 54 drachmas 3 1/2 obols, including the fees.

Paragraph 3, lines 13-14

"If anyone gains possession of a slave in consequence of a higher bid or a counterbid, he shall pay to the city another brokerage fee."

For the verb κατέχειν as used for the victor in the bidding in the case of the tax farming privilege, see U.P.Z. 112 (=P. Paris 62) III 11 ff., ἐὰν δέ τινες τῶν κατασχόντων τὰς ὠνὰς μὴ διεγγυήσωσιν ἐν τῶι ὡρισμένωι χρόνωι. The auctioning system, as it applied to the tax farming sale, has been known from the passage just quoted. For the auctioning of lands under heritable lease it has been known from P. Eleph. 14 (= Wilcken, *Chrest.* 340), and from the Theban bank documents published by Wilcken.[31] Briefly restated in accordance with Wilcken's discussion (in U.P.Z. I p. 515) of the passage quoted above from P. Paris 62, the steps in the Ptolemaic system of auctioning were the following: The highest bid made on the day of auction might be overbid (ὑπερβάλλειν), by any amount desired, for a period of ten days. After the acceptance of this overbid, the entering of a second higher bid was permitted. This second higher bid must exceed the overbid (ὑπερβολή) by at least ten per cent.

Two additions to the phraseology of the auctioning system are provided by P. Col. Inv. 480, in ἀνθυπερβολή and προπρατικόν. ἀνθυπερβολή expresses simply and clearly the idea of the "counterbid" against the higher bid which had been provisionally accepted and posted.[32] The technical steps, in their substantive forms, were πρᾶσις, ὑπερβολή (ὑπερβόλιον in P. Par. 63 VIII 8, 10), ἀνθυπερβολή, corresponding to πράττειν, ὑπερβάλλειν, ἀνθυπερβάλλειν. The identity of the προπρατικόν with the προπωλητικόν of line 10 is clear from the context; and it is further indicated by the identification of προπράτωρ and προπώλης in Pollux VII, 11-12: ὁ δὲ τοῖς

---

[31] "Aktenstücke aus der königlichen Bank zu Theben," in *Abh. Berl. Akad.*, 1886. Cf. Wilcken, *Gr. Ostraka* I, p. 525, who projects a re-edition with new readings and further restorations of documents I-IV, on the auctions, for the second volume of U.P.Z.

[32] The verb ἀνθυπερβάλλειν occurs in Josephus, *Ant. Jud.* 16. 7, 2 where its meaning is taken over from the tax bidding procedure.

πιπράσκουσι προξενῶν, προπράτωρ, ὡς Δείναρχος καὶ Ἰσαῖος, προπώλην δὲ Ἀριστοφάνης αὐτὸν εἶπε, καὶ προπωλοῦντα Πλάτων.

The wording of the διάγραμμα must, I think, be interpreted in the sense that the purchaser who obtained a slave by overbidding an original bid paid the brokerage fee (προπρατικόν) twice and the person who bought one by a counterbid against an overbid paid it three times.[33] This seems a reasonable arrangement in that there would be clerical and other office work demanded both in the case of the overbid and of the counterbid.

Whether the tax on the sale falls upon the purchaser or the vendor is not specifically stated; but it is to be assumed that the purchaser would bear it, just as in paragraph 2, seeing that the vendor was required to pay only a part of the tax even under the arrangements in paragraph 1. This decision is also indicated by the statement that the final victor in the bidding, the purchaser, is to pay the additional brokerage fee.

Paragraph 4, lines 15-18

"Upon those sold through the *praktores xenikon* the purchasers shall pay, per mina, 19 drachmas, and as crier's fee a one per cent tax, 1 drachma, and for the *dorea* as clerical fee, per head, 1 drachma."

As stated before, a different organization was here employed for the sale of slaves from that used under the voluntary sales contemplated in the first three paragraphs. This paragraph deals with the slaves which came into the hands of the officials of the state tribunals in consequence of court judgments through execution on the property of defeated litigants or for fines imposed upon them. The *praktores xenikon*, who executed judgment, also *conducted the auctions in these cases*. The brokerage fee does not appear. In addition to the one per cent *ad valorem* fee in the voluntary sales, here given its specific name as the fee paid for crier's services, a clerical fee is here exacted, which is a specific charge of 1 drachma on each slave sold. This clerical fee (lines 17-18, cf. lines 21-22) was now the source of income which made the royal grant to Dicaearchus, instead of the one per cent tax of paragraphs 1-3 which had formerly been paid to him. The brokerage fee of 4 drachmas 1 obol does not appear.

---

[33] Had it been exacted only with one of these two, not with each, ἢ ἀνθυπερβολῆς would simply have been omitted.

In the cases of these forced sales on judgments, which are handled by the *praktores xenikon*, the tax farmers must, of course, have collected the taxes and fees *from the purchasers*, since the bailiffs had made attachment upon the slaves, and the former owners were no longer concerned in the sale.[34]

Paragraph 5, lines 19-23

"Upon those being sold in consequence of debts to the royal treasury the purchasers shall pay, per mina, 16 drachmas 5 obols, and as crier's fee a one per cent tax, 1 drachma, and as clerical fee for the *dorea* of Dicaearchus, per head, 1 drachma."

The tax required from the buyers who purchased slaves from properties attached for debts to the fiscal department is 2 1/6 drachmas less per slave than that exacted on slaves sold through the judicial department, in satisfaction of court decisions, by execution on the property of unsuccessful litigants. The difference is about twelve per cent. The Zois papyri,[35] which give a concrete example of a sale of a garden $\pi\rho\grave{o}s$ $\beta\alpha\sigma\iota\lambda\iota\kappa\acute{a}$ at forced public auction, may help to explain this difference.

The transactions recorded in the Zois papyri cover the years 29-32 of a Ptolemy of the second century who is identified by Wilcken as Philometor rather than Euergetes II.[36] A man named Dorion had contracted, along with others, for the collection of the natron tax for the year 29, and a woman named Thanubis had gone upon his bond to the amount of 11 talents 4000 copper drachmas as surety for payment to the state, giving in as security a garden which belonged to her. As Dorion did not pay, and Thanubis could not pay more than a small amount of the debt, the garden was attached for forced sale by the government. An arrangement was made by Thanubis that her daughter, Zois, should bid in the garden, without opposition, on the basis that Zois would pay the debt to the state in four annual installments, assisted by payment of a small portion of the debt by Thanubis. The docu-

[34] Note also that in the next paragraph, according to the interpretation which has been adopted here, it is the buyers who pay the taxes.

[35] Wilcken has republished them, for the first time giving the complete readings of the double documents, in U.P.Z. I 114.

[36] Under this dating, strongly supported by proposed identification of three of the officials whose names occur in the Zois papyri with officials of the same name who appear in other dated papyri (see U.P.Z. I p. 524), the years are 153-148 B.C.

ments recorded the complete payment of the four installments by Zois. In making her payments Zois was charged, pro rata on each installment, a 1 2/3 per cent fee (ἐξηκοστή) and a one per cent fee (ἑκατοστή).[37] In P. Eleph. 14, 11, of the third century B.C., the fee charges are "the 1 2/3 per cent fee and the herald's fee on the whole amount, the one one-thousandth." Ulrich Wilcken has suggested, though tentatively (apparently because of the tremendous difference in the size of the fee) that the *hekatoste* of the Zois papyri must be the herald's fee of P. Eleph. 14.[38] This is supported by the statement, in P. Zois I 25-27, that the auction sales had been called out by the herald Demetrius.

Paragraph 5 of P. Col. Inv. 480 stands between P. Elephantine 14, of 223-222 B.C., and P. Zois, in its content as well as in time. P. Eleph. 14 is similar to P. Col. Inv. 480 in that it, too, is an ordinance; but it is one which regulates the auctioning of those private holdings of debtors to the state which are subject to lease—not to sale. P. Zois presents a concrete case of the *application* of the existing ordinance on the auctioning of properties attached by the state, and differs further from P. Col. Inv. 480, paragraph 5, in respect to the object of the sale, namely, real estate rather than slaves. The analogy of the enforced sales by auction in each case is nevertheless close. The one per cent fee for herald's service of P. Col. Inv. 480, 20-21 (κηρύκειον ἑκατοστήν) gives complete support to Wilcken's suggestion that the *hekatoste* of P. Zois must be the herald's fee. Furthermore it strongly suggests that the 1 2/3 per cent fee (ἐξηκοστή) of P. Zois is a clerical fee, corresponding to the *graphion* of paragraphs 4-5 of P. Col. Inv. 480. The 1 2/3 per cent fee of P. Zois is, however, much higher than the *graphion* rate of P. Col. Inv. 480, which is merely one per cent per slave sold. This would be less than one per cent *ad valorem*, because the supposition throughout the Columbia ordinance seems to be that, in all cases, the sale price of the slaves would be above one mina each. The reason for the difference in the amount of the clerical fee in the two cases might well be explained as an advancement in all the clerical fees in the forty odd years which elapsed between the passage of the *diagramma* on the slaves and the Zois case, or as an original disparity in the amount of the clerical fee upon real estate sales by government auction and

[37] P. Zois I (=U.P.Z. 114), line 4; II, line 5.
[38] U.P.Z. 114, note 4.

of that upon slave sales, due to a difference in the necessary amount of clerical work involved in the two cases.

Paragraph 6, lines 24-26

"Upon persons enslaved for debt, as many as, when free, may have . . . the debt, they shall collect from the lender, per mina, 5 drachmas 1 obol, and from the borrower 5 drachmas 1 obol, total per mina 10 drachmas 2 obols, and as clerical fee, per head, 1 drachma."

The loss of the verb at the beginning of line 24, which would have added greatly to the knowledge of execution upon the person in the Ptolemaic period, is a serious one. It is all the more to be regretted because the restoration of the lacuna at the beginning of line 27 and the meaning of paragraph 7 depend largely upon a correct restoration in line 24. The following analysis is necessarily offered with no positiveness as to its correctness, but in the hope of laying a basis for a more convincing solution of the problems involved.

Paragraphs 4 and 5 dealt, respectively, with taxes on the sales of slaves in execution upon the property of unsuccessful litigants and with those on slaves sold in consequence of debts to the crown. Paragraph 6 deals with debtor slaves ($\tau\hat{\omega}\nu$ $\dot{\upsilon}\pi o\chi\rho\dot{\epsilon}\omega\nu$ $\sigma\omega\mu\dot{\alpha}\tau\omega\nu$). I have not found the combination of $\dot{\upsilon}\pi\acute{o}\chi\rho\epsilon\alpha$ $\sigma\acute{\omega}\mu\alpha\tau\alpha$ used heretofore in the papyri.[39] As has been explained above, the persons in this classification must have been regarded, from the standpoint of the fiscal department certainly, though perhaps not in the complete legal sense, as slaves, since they appear in this ordinance upon slaves. The grammatical necessity of the indefinite conditional with $\pi\rho\dot{\alpha}\xi o\nu\tau\alpha\iota$ (line 24) will not permit the reading $\ddot{o}\sigma\alpha$ $\dot{\alpha}\nu\epsilon\lambda\epsilon\dot{\upsilon}\theta\epsilon\rho\alpha$ in the place of $\ddot{o}\sigma\alpha$ $\ddot{\alpha}\nu$ $\dot{\epsilon}\lambda\epsilon\dot{\upsilon}\theta\epsilon\rho\alpha$. $\dot{\alpha}\nu\epsilon\lambda\epsilon\dot{\upsilon}\theta\epsilon\rho\alpha$ would, also, constitute a useless repetition of the fact that they were unfree, expressed immediately before in $\dot{\upsilon}\pi o\chi\rho\dot{\epsilon}\omega\nu$ $\sigma\omega\mu\dot{\alpha}\tau\omega\nu$ and implied by the fact of their incorporation in this ordinance upon the slaves. The passage seems to demand an action of these debtors which took place when they were still free, intervening between their status as free men and their status as slaves[40]—an action which had to do with their

---

[39] In the sixth century Byzantine document, P. Masp. 67022, *verso*, 6a, $\kappa\tau\hat{\eta}\mu\alpha$ $\dot{\upsilon}\pi\acute{o}\chi\rho[\epsilon\omega\nu]$ appears.

[40] This seemed to me to eliminate the possibility of $\dot{\alpha}\pi o\delta\hat{\omega}\tau\alpha\iota$ or a like verb indicating that they had paid the debt. $\dot{\epsilon}\gamma\gamma\upsilon\hat{\alpha}\nu$ in this passage would be quite unusual, according to Partsch, *Bürgschaftsrecht*, p. 63, and particularly so because of the presence of $\dot{\epsilon}\alpha\upsilon[\tau\dot{\alpha}$.

transfer of status. I have therefore suggested above (see note 24 to the Greek text) the two possible readings, ἐαυ-[τὰ προσδῶται πρὸς or ὑποθῆται εἰς] τὸ χρέος, with preference for προσδῶται. Cf. B.G.U. IV 1138 (of 19/18 B.C.), where a prison guard bears witness that one Papias had been given up to him in satisfaction of a debt, περὶ το(ῦ) παραδεδόσθαι αὐτῶι τὸν Παπίαν πρὸς τὰ(s) το(ῦ) ἀργυ(ρίου) (δραχμὰs) (χιλίαs) (ἐξακοσίαs).[41]

τὸν δανειζόμε[νο]ν of line 25, the borrower, is, in definite application to a single person, one of the "debtor slaves" referred to in the general heading of the paragraph as τῶν ὑποχρέων σωμάτων. As I interpret the paragraph, it deals with the debtors who voluntarily submit themselves to bondage in cases of unpaid debts which were pledged by their own persons. In most instances, as in B.G.U. IV 1138, they would obtain an ἔγγυος who would advance the money for the liquidation of the debt. The idea that the cases here considered were settled by liquidation of the debt is suggested by the fact that the borrower, i.e., the "debtor slave," must pay his share of the sale tax imposed. The lack of the one per cent tax for herald's fee indicates that no auction sale was contemplated in these cases. However these cases may have been settled, the state regarded such transactions as the equivalent of slave transfers by sale, and placed a sale tax upon them. This was light in comparison with the taxes in the regular commercial sales and in the sales brought about by court or fiscal action. As against the *ad valorem* of 17 5/6 per cent (plus 4 drachmas 1 obol on each slave) of paragraph 1 we here have a total *ad valorem* of 10 1/3 per cent of the debt plus a clerical fee of 1 drachma per head. The 10 1/3 per cent tax falls in equal division upon creditor and debtor. As in paragraph 1, both the incidence of the tax and its low rate correspond to advantages to the two parties concerned in the transaction and to an advantage for the government in the minimal amount of its trouble and of the services which it must render. It is not clearly stated upon whom the clerical fee of 1 drachma falls; but I judge, by the nearer position of τὸν δανειζόμενον, that it would rest upon the borrower. This allocation receives some support from the arrangement in the commercial sale in paragraph 1, where the seller pays the one per cent fee. Here the borrower (= debtor) had, in the event, sold his services by pledging his person against the

---

[41] Cf. H. Lewald, *Zur Personalexekution im Recht der Papyri*, Leipzig, 1910, pp. 34-36.

debt; and he may therefore be regarded as corresponding in position to the vendor of paragraph 1. There is no definite indication that, in these arrangements for debtor slaves, the clerical fee went to the *dorea* of Dicaearchus.

Paragraph 7, lines 27-28

". . . in relation to the debt, they shall collect [from the purchaser?] . . . drachmas 5 obols and as one per cent tax 1 drachma [and as clerical fee, per head, 1 drachma?]."

In the sequence of the types of sales of slaves which the *diagramma* is concerned with, this section must refer to the "debtor slaves" (ὑπόχρεα σώματα) who have not been able to obtain a liquidation of their debt and are eventually sold as slaves in satisfaction of the lender's claim. Because of the certain reading of the letters -ην in line 28, the traces of the remaining letters, and the requirements of the space, the reading καὶ ἑκατοστήν seems to be the only possible one. Apparently it is the κηρύκειον ἑκατοστήν of lines 17 and 21-22; and the sale would be carried out as a compulsory auction sale. By comparison with section 4, upon the slaves sold by the *praktores xenikon*, it seems to be clear that the *praktores xenikon did not conduct these sales*.

The γραφῖον did not go to Dicaearchus, by any definite statement of the text, in the case of the debtor slaves of paragraph 6. The same doubt applies to the question whether the *hekatoste* of this section was paid to him. The 1 drachma clerical fee (the *graphion*) has been added by me in line 30 because it has appeared in each of the three paragraphs, 4-6, in which the city brokerage tax did not appear.

DICAEARCHUS AND THE *Dorea*

In the explanation of the date given to P. Col. Inv. 480, reasons were offered for the assumption that Dicaearchus, who received as his grant from the king of Egypt certain fees from the sales of slaves, was an Aetolian mercenary known to us from brief comments of Polybius and Diodorus. An excerpt from Diodorus states that Philip, king of the Macedonians, persuaded Dicaearchus the Aetolian, a man of daring character, to sail the Aegean as a pirate. Philip gave him twenty ships, with orders to exact tribute from the islands (the Cyclades, according to Polybius) and to give aid to the Cretans in the war of Philip against the Rhodians. In accordance with these orders Dicaearchus carried on piracy against the merchants and collected money by plundering the islands.[42]

This action of Philip V, who secretly encouraged the piracies of the Cretans and directed them chiefly against the Rhodians, the constant enemies of piracy in the Aegean Sea, began in 205 or in 204 B.C.[43] The connection of Dicaearchus with these events, as a piratical plunderer according to Polybius and Diodorus, is to be placed in these years,[44] with the possibility of an extension into the year 203.[45]

Beyond the information about him which is brought by P. Col. Inv. 480 the only news we have of Dicaearchus touches upon his blatant display of irreverence toward the gods and the manner of his death. Plutarch relates that in his activities in the Cyclades, of 205 or 204 B.C., he was accustomed, wherever he put in at a harbor, to build two altars, one to Irreverence and one to Lawlessness, and to make sacrifice to them and worship them as gods. Polybius implies that this action had the intent of putting fear into gods and men.[46] It may be that Dicaearchus was a man of utterly vapid ruthlessness who was willing to offend the religious sensibilities of his political opponents to no good end. But the political position which he obviously attained in Egypt does not support this view. It seems better, therefore, to find the explanation of his otherwise senseless proceeding, in respect to his public affront to the accepted religious forms, in his desire to make the Islanders amenable to his exactions by a preliminary display of offensive impiety and suggested savagery. At best it throws an ill light upon his understanding of the psychology and the prejudices of the people with whom he had to deal.

In Polybius' account Dicaearchus appears later in the service of Ptolemy V, where he met his death on the order of the then regent, Aristomenes the Acarnanian. He was the only one of the group of the mercenary leaders

---

[42] Diodorus XXVIII 1. Cf. Polybius' account (XVIII 7-8) of the death by torture meted out in Egypt to Dicaearchus as the infliction of a fitting punishment upon him and a common vengeance on behalf of all the Greeks.

[43] See the argument of M. Holleaux in *Revue des Études Grecques* XXXIII (1920), pp. 223-247.

[44] *Ibid.*, p. 246.

[45] But not later, see Holleaux, *loc. cit.*, pp. 225-226.

[46] Polybius XVIII 54.

arrested and killed at that time, presumably on the charge of conspiracy, who suffered his death after tortures.[47]

The last five years of the life of Dicaearchus may be followed with a relative degree of chronological accuracy. His activities and his fate are commingled with those of his fellow Aetolian, the *condottiere* Scopas of Trichonion, notorious for his financial greed, according to the account of him given by Polybius. For the chronological arrangement of the activities of Scopas and Dicaearchus, we have three events which are fixed in definite years: (1) the service of Dicaearchus with Philip V against the Rhodians in 205 or 204 B.C.; (2) the second recruiting of Aetolian mercenaries by Scopas for the Egyptian service against Antiochus III of Syria in 200-199 B.C.,[48] and (3) the deaths of Scopas, his family and his adherents, including Dicaearchus, shortly before the official enthronement of Ptolemy V Epiphanes, which occurred in November of 197 B.C. For the hiring of Scopas by the Egyptian government and his first mission into Aetolia for recruitment of soldiers "with an abundance of money for the advance payments," see Polybius XV 25. 16. This mission has been dated by M. Holleaux at the end of the year 203 B.C.[49] The acceptance of service with the Egyptian army by Dicaearchus and his continuance in that service are easily explained. It would ill accord with the Roman policy, either at the time of the Roman preparations for the war with Philip or during that war, to permit an Aetolian who had so recently been a hireling of Philip to gain or hold any position of prominence in his native land in 201 or thereafter. To this is to be added the consideration that the campaign of Dicaearchus in 205 or 204 was directed against the Rhodians, that they were already exercising a decisive influence before the Roman Senate in 201 B.C.,[50] and that Dicaearchus had made himself offensive to the Greek world at large.

[47] Polybius, *loc. cit.*, had previously stated the accusations against the mercenaries, but the passage is lost: XVIII 54, 2, παραπλήσιος ἡ κατηγορία πάντων τοῖς ἄρτι ῥηθεῖσι.

[48] Recounted by Livy, XXXI 43, 4. The date is fixed by the *strategeia* of Damocritus of Calydon in Aetolia, which, in Livy's account, falls in the year 200-199 B.C. See Haussoullier in *Bull. Corr. Hell.* V (1881) p. 409, and M. Holleaux, *Klio* VIII (1906) pp. 277-278.

[49] *Ibid.* Cf. Niese II p. 604, who places the engagement of Scopas by Egypt in 205-204 (p. 563), but accords with Holleaux in the date of the first recruiting mission. It must be placed before the death of the regent Agathocles, which may be dated, with much probability, in 202 B.C.

[50] See M. Holleaux, *Rome, la Grèce et les monarchies hellénistiques*, p. 328, n. 2.

The close connection of Dicaearchus with Scopas is certain. They were both Aetolians and no doubt known to each other during the early and brilliant career of Scopas in his native land. That Dicaearchus was an adherent of Scopas in Egypt is proven by his death in consequence of the court struggle which destroyed them both upon the same night.[51] There are several reasons for placing the beginning of their Egyptian connection and the enlistment of Dicaearchus in the service of Ptolemy V in the year 203 B.C. rather than during the second recruiting mission of Scopas in 200-199 B.C. The period of the service of Dicaearchus in Egypt must be long enough to allow for the allocation to him of a one per cent fee on certain types of slave sales and for the change from this to the clerical fee on another kind of slave sale.[52] Had he been recruited in 200-199 B.C., allowing some time for the transference of the one per cent fee to him and the change to the *graphion* as his royal grant, he could have held them for only two years, or less. The earlier date permits five years for the changes involved. The second reason lies in the situation in Aetolia, mentioned above, which was decidedly unfavorable for Dicaearchus and must have made him amenable to an Egyptian offer immediately upon the cessation of his piratical service under Philip. In either case the connection of his Egyptian career with that of Scopas is the same.

The greed for gain, which was marked in the character of Scopas in his lifetime, was attested after his death by the riches in money and furnishings found in his house.[53] Indeed there is small room for doubt that these mercenary generals and their captains who settled upon Egypt in the period of the minority of Ptolemy V (203-197) fed abundantly at the trough of the state. At his enlistment for the Egyptian service Scopas had received, if we may believe Polybius, the enormous salary of ten minas per day, his subordinates each one mina per day.[54] Polybius mentions one Charimortus, not

---

[51] Polybius XVIII 54, 6-7.

[52] The method of designating one of the fees as "the one per cent fee formerly *collected* for the *dorea* of Dicaearchus"—not "payable to the *dorea*"—suggests the probability that the fees here recorded constituted the whole of his grant, each in its turn.

[53] Polybius XVIII 55, 1-2; cf. XIII 2, 1. Polybius uses an expression which means that he pillaged the state as a housebreaking burglar would have done it, ἄρδην ἐξετοιχωρύχησε τὴν βασιλείαν.

[54] Polybius XIII 3. Not while campaigning only, but τῆς ἡμέρας ἐκάστης.

Dicaearchus, as the special aid of Scopas in his "burglarizing of the kingdom." Yet it was Dicaearchus alone who was subjected to torture by the rack and to the ignominy of scourging to death. Polybius took a grim satisfaction in the manner of his death as "a fitting and general punishment in behalf of all the Greeks." His words may mean that the general hatred against Dicaearchus among the Greeks at large motivated the atrocious manner of his death. This would imply that Aristomenes, the regent, and his clique were playing their political game with an eye to the position of Egypt in the Greek world. This may be true; but the situation existing at that time in Egypt was a troubled one. It resulted in the victory of the nationalist sentiment as led by the Egyptian priesthood and as expressed in the decree promulgated by the synod of the Egyptian priesthood held at Memphis on March 27, 196 B.C.[55] It seems more reasonable to search for a nearer motive for the especial hatred displayed toward Dicaearchus, perhaps in his use in Egypt of methods as offensive to the Egyptian nationalists as those which he followed in the Aegean in 205-204 B.C. were offensive to the Greeks. The manner of his death would, in that case, have been a concession to the nationalist feeling in Egypt by the opposing group of Greeks who caused the downfall of Scopas.

The exact fees which Dicaearchus received as his grant were these: at first a one per cent fee on all slave sales consummated between private individuals (paragraphs 1-3); later, a clerical fee of one drachma on each slave that was sold by forced public auction on the part of the state (paragraphs 4-5).[56] The fact that he received these fees as a grant can not be regarded, of itself, as something sufficiently offensive to the sensibilities of the Egyptians to explain the hatred shown in the manner of his execution. Precedents are known for the *dorea* as a pure money grant[57]—and in one case precisely for the allocation of the clerical fee ($\gamma\rho\alpha\varphi\varepsilon\hat{\iota}o\nu$) as a *dorea*. These are P. Hibeh

[55] The Rosetta Stone decree. See, for the English translation, Bevan, *History of Egypt under the Ptolemaic Dynasty*, pp. 263 ff.

[56] The *graphion* of paragraphs 6 and 7 may possibly have been assigned to Dicaearchus. But as it is explicitly stated in paragraphs 1, 4 and 5 (and to be assumed for paragraphs 2 and 3) that the fees went to Dicaearchus, and it is not so stated in paragraph 6, I have assumed that the fees upon debtor slaves were not included in his later grant.

[57] See Rostovtzeff, *Large Estate*, p. 45 and note 49; and cf. in P. Hibeh 66 the discussion of the editors in note to lines 1-2.

66, of 228-227 B.C.; a Trinity College papyrus (published as P. Petrie III 53s) dated in year 16 of Euergetes I;[58] and a bank receipt for the sale tax on 11 5/8 arurae of arable land in the Pathyrite nome, of 209 B.C.[59] P. Hibeh 66 is a letter from one Protarchus to Clitarchus, head of a royal bank in the Coite district, stating that Protarchus had contracted for the collection of a 1 1/2 per cent fee (otherwise undefined), taking it over from the tax-farmers of the *dorea*. He asks the banker, since the five per cent tax in that region was paid in to him, to order his agents to collect also the fees which Protarchus had contracted for. Clearly the collection of the taxes allocated to a definite grant (*dorea*, otherwise undefined in this letter) was sold here *en bloc* to a group of tax contractors, who sublet them piecemeal to secondary tax farmers, of whom Protarchus was one. For our purpose the important feature is that in 228-227 B.C. definite money revenues of the state are found grouped as a *dorea*. It is impossible to tell whether this tax *dorea* at the time of the letter had reverted to the state or not. It might have done so and might still have retained the designation *dorea*.

Because my interpretation of P. Petrie III 53s differs in certain particulars from any that I have yet seen, the document is here presented in full: μερας ("probably the end of ἡμέρας," say the editors) κ προστάγματα βασιλέως Πτολεμαίου. ἀφείκαμεν δὲ καί τὸ γραφῖον τῶν Αἰγυπτίων συγγραφῶν, τὸ δὲ ἀπὸ [τ]ούτων πρότερον πεῖπτον διδόναι παρ' αὐτοῦ τοῖς ἔχουσι τὴν δωρεάν (followed by date). The first sentence, ἀφείκαμεν δὲ, etc., has generally been explained with the meaning, "I have remitted also the clerical fee upon the Egyptian contracts," that is, those contracts written in demotic.[60] This interpretation seems impossible to follow in view of the second sentence, in which the general meaning certainly is that the revenue from the clerical fee upon the Egyptian contracts was to go to those who held the *dorea*, *i.e.*, the grant of this fee. The document, it seems to me, is an extract from a decree of the king,[61] sent out, in a highly abbreviated form, to the nome

[58] Wilcken in U.P.Z. I p. 608.

[59] Preisigke, *Sammelbuch* 5729 = *Proceed. Soc. Bibl.* XIV (1891) p. 61. Cf. Wilcken, *Gr. Ostraka* I p. 362. In the light of P. Col. Inv. 480, Wilcken's explanation of this *dorea, loc. cit.*, will scarcely hold.

[60] So interpreted also by Wilcken in U.P.Z. I p. 508.

[61] No doubt emanating really from the office of the dioecetes, as Wilcken states, *loc. cit.*

officials. ἀφείκαμεν is to be understood in the sense "I have set aside";[62] and the second sentence must have read, in full, somewhat as follows: τὸ δὲ ἀπὸ τούτων πρότερον πίπτον (scil. εἰς τὸ βασιλικὸν) διδόναι παρ' αὑτοῦ[63] τοῖς ἔχουσι τὴν δωρεάν: "Assign the revenues formerly accruing from them (to the basilikon) from it (the basilikon) to those who hold the grant (dorea)." The original decree would have been directed to the officials of the central bureau of the treasury who would pay the dorea to its recipient. The abbreviated statement of its content, as noted down by the nome officials, served as an order to them to account separately and under a new heading for the clerical fees upon the contracts drawn up in demotic, as these fees came in to them from the tax farmers. Previously the clerical fee had, no doubt, been accounted for in the archival bookkeeping of the nomes under a separate heading, such as τὸ γραφῖον τῶν Αἰγυπτίων συγγραφῶν. After receiving the order announcing its transfer, the officials must have reported it, in their annual accounting to the central bureau, under a general rubric headed δωρεά (or δωρεαί), probably indicating also, as formerly, its specific source as the γραφῖον τῶν Αἰγυπτίων συγγραφῶν.

The bank receipt of 209 B.C., quoted above, for the sale tax on arable land,[64] mentions also a fee called simply "dorea." The bank had accepted, for the contractor of the tax on real estate sales (ἐγκύκλιον), the amount of the sale tax and two fees, the dorea and the chalkiaia. Evidently, therefore, the bank on its account books showed this tax and the two fees under the three headings ἐγκύκλιον, δωρεά (obviously a clerical fee, or some similar fee, used as a grant), and χαλκιαία.

An unpublished and fragmentary Columbia papyrus, P. Col. Inv. 228 verso, lines 12-13, mentions a dorea, which is unquestionably a money grant. Lines 17-19 read:

τοῖς τὴν δωρεὰν ἔχουσιν [
ἀπὸ τῆς μνᾶς (δραχμὰς) β. ἐὰν δ[ὲ μὴ ἀπο-
γράψωνται ἐν τῶι γεγ[

---

[62] As in P. Oxy, 932.5; B.G.U. 98, 12; P. Teb. 421, 9-10.

[63] διδόναι παρ αὑτοῦ. Infinitive with imperative force. Cf. the explanation of the editors of P. Hib. 66, note to 1-2, which is open to several objections, notably that πρότερον πίπτον διδόναι παρ' αὑτοῦ can scarcely mean that the proceeds previously derived from it (the tax) are to be transferred to the holders of the dorea. The proceeds were still derived from this tax.

[64] Preisigke, Sammelbuch 5729.

This is, therefore, a two per cent fee the returns from which are granted to a group of people. The fragment is dated in the nineteenth year and seems to be of the reign of Ptolemy III. The recto is dated by the basket-bearer of Arsinoe Philadelphus, whose name is Arsinoe, daughter of Polemocrates, as of the year 3 of Ptolemy III.[65]

To this information upon the *dorea* as money grant is to be added an ostrakon from Upper Egypt published by Ernst Kühn, the writing of which is dim and partially lost.[65a] The script is of the third century B.C. It is a state bank receipt, dated in year 15, for money paid "into the *dorea* of Agathocles."[65b] The identification of this Agathocles as the favorite of Ptolemy IV Philopator was made with reservation by Kühn. Since Agathocles was put to death in 202 B.C. and we now have the money *dorea* of Dicaearchus assured by P. Col. Inv. 480 for the years immediately following that date, the identification may well be accepted as certain. Kühn refers to a Strassburg ostrakon which records a payment also "into the *dorea* of Agathocles of the [ ] from wine and fruit trees" (εἰς τὴν 'Αγαθοκλείους [...] δωρεά (*sic*) τοῦ οἴνου [..] κ(αὶ) ἀκροδρύων). This receipt Kühn dates as probably of the first century B.C.[65c] With the exception of the Strassburg ostrakon the use of money revenue as a *dorea* in Egypt is thus far attested only for the reigns of Ptolemies III Euergetes, IV Philopator and V Epiphanes.

THE *Diagramma* AS A SOURCE OF LAW

The Columbia document is the most considerable direct extract from a Ptolemaic *diagramma* which has thus far appeared except the shattered *diagramma* on banks in P. Rev. 73-78. It adds several points of interest to the existing knowledge of this type of Ptolemaic legislation, which has been

[65] Walter Otto, *Priester und Tempel*, Leipzig, 1908, II p. 325.

[65a] Wilhelm Schubart und Ernst Kühn, *Papyri und Ostraka der Ptolemäerzeit* (B.G.U. VI), Berlin, 1922, no. 1415.

[65b] (ἔτους) ιε Μεχειρ ς τέτακ[ται] Ὧρος εἰς τὴν 'Αγαθοκ(λέους) δωρεὰν τοτυτεξ[ ] κ.τ.λ.

[65c] If Kühn's dating (by the script presumably) is correct, the old name of the account of these taxes in the finance records must have been long retained as "the *dorea* of Agathocles." Cf. the possibility regarding the account "*dorea* of Dicaearchus" discussed on page 1, note 3. This assumption eliminates the necessity of predicating another Agathocles of important position in Egypt who would be otherwise unknown.

less clearly defined than the other three important sources of law (the *nomoi*, the *prostagmata* and the *diorthomata*).[66]

As to the form used in the *diagramma* on slaves, the mild future is employed throughout in the basic paragraphs stating the general obligations of the tax contractors or tax payers.[67] There is no use of the imperative, which is also avoided in the directions upon the leasing of all the taxes of the Oxyrhynchite nome in P. Paris 62 (= U.P.Z. 112).[68] Special provisions, or variations and exceptions from these basic paragraphs, are couched in the conditional form, introduced by ἐὰν δέ τις (P. Col. Inv. 480, paragraphs 2-3). A similar usage appears in a citation from a *diagramma* on the judiciary in P. Petrie 36a, *verso* (= Mitteis, *Chrest.* 5). The *diagramma* from which this quotation comes seemingly dealt with the assignments of cases to their proper courts. The paragraph is thus quoted: ὑπάρχοντας γὰρ ἐν τ[ῶ]ι διαγράμματι, "ἐὰν δέ τινες . . . ἐνκαλέσωσιν," lines 11-14. It made special provision for reference to the dioecetes, or to others by his delegation, of complaints against the activities of officials of the finance department.[69] In the shattered *diagramma*-ordinance upon banks, incorporated in the Revenue Laws, the use of the future in sections 73-74 changes, however, to the imperative in sections 75-78. In P. Rev. 76, the use of the imperative is particularly to be noted. That section deals with the discount rate between copper and silver in the bank monopolies and is, therefore, in content, peculiarly characteristic of the *diagrammata* known to us. As Wilcken has pointed out,[70] hard and fast rules cannot as yet be made regarding the forms of speech employed in *diagrammata* and laws (*nomoi*).

As the information upon the Egyptian *diagrammata* now stands we know two types: those dealing with the courts, especially those defining the methods of execution upon property; and those of an economic character, dealing with

[66] See Wilcken, note to U.P.Z. I 112, 6-8.

[67] πράξονται is used with the tax farmers as subject in lines 3, 24 and 27 of P. Col. Inv. 480, πραχθήσονται with the tax payers as subject in lines 16 (as emended) and 19.

[68] In P. Paris 62 the imperative occurs only in the direct admonition of the King to the bidders for the tax farming privilege, lines 3-13. Elsewhere the future prevails. According to Wilcken's dating, P. Paris 62 is of 203-202 B.C. (U.P.Z. I pp. 502 f.), only a few years earlier than P. Col. Inv. 480.

[69] P. M. Meyer, *Klio* VII 289, note 2.

[70] U.P.Z. I pp. 501 f.

the relations between officials and subjects.[71] The *diagrammata* give the normal law in accordance with which the Ptolemaic subjects lived; they took precedence over the *nomoi*,[72] and they were subject to frequent change.

The following specific cases of *diagrammata* of the second type, regulating the tax arrangements (therefore similar to P. Col. Inv. 480) and other relations between the Ptolemaic officials and the subjects of the realm, have already appeared:

(1) *Diagramma* on the banks (διάγραμμα τραπεζῶν).[73]

(2) *Diagramma* on the oil monopoly.

a) One clause of this ordinance, in the form in which it was published in the year 26 of Philadelphus to apply to year 27, changed the price which the contractors of the oil monopoly were to pay to the cultivators of the oil plants for the produce, in case the seed were prepared for grinding at the government oil factory.[74] It is certain that *diagrammata* on this particular subject of the price changed frequently, though not necessarily annually.[75]

b) A clause of the oil *diagramma*, connected with the one above, fixed for the tax contractors the conversion value of a 2 drachma tax on sesame and a 1 drachma tax on croton, which they collected from the cultivators, into terms of the produce itself, that is, into sesame and croton seed: λαμβανέτωσαν . . . εἰς τὰς δύο δραχμὰς τὰς λογ[ευο]μένας ἀπὸ τοῦ σησάμου καὶ τὴν (δραχμὴν) α [του κ]ρότωνος σήσαμον καὶ κρότωνα τιμῆς τ[ῆς ἐν] τῶι διαγράμματι γεγραμμένης, ἀργύριον δὲ μὴ πρασσέσθωσαν.[76] This provision must have been altered frequently (though by no means annually) to meet changes in the value of money and other economic shifts.

c) In another clause of the oil monopoly *diagramma*, the price of the oil (or of the seed?)[77] was fixed, in the relations of the oil workers to the government oil factories.

[71] See *Dikaiomata*, pp. 42-43; note to P. Teb. I 5, 264.

[72] E. Bickermann, *Archiv* VIII p. 227.

[73] P. Rev. 73-78.

[74] P. Rev. 39, 1-7; cf. 53, 11.

[75] Grenfell has suggested as probable (P. Rev. p. 152) that the changes were annual.

[76] P. Rev. 39, 13-18. See the explanation of the clause of the σιτολογικὸν διάγραμμα on conversion value referred to in P. Col. Inv. 270 in *Memoirs Am. Acad. in Rome*, VI (1927).

[77] P. Rev. 48, 19-49, 2. These lines are badly broken.

d) The sale price of the manufactured oil, paid by the dealers, was fixed in the *diagramma*. This must have also been a changing regulation.[78]

(3) *Diagramma* relating to the government monopoly of fine cloths, which fixed the price of *byssos* cloths and certain tow and wool products.[79]

(4) *Diagramma* fixing the amount of a tax (?) upon natron, manufactured into soap in the government monopoly.[80]

(5) *Diagramma* on the grain payments. From this ordinance two clauses have been determined. The one provided that grain payments for rent were to be made at the local government granary.[81] The second fixed the conversion value of wheat into terms of coined money.[82] The latter of these provisions would be subject to frequent change.

(6) *Diagramma* fixing the interest rate on loans at two per cent per month. This is known from numerous contracts of loan falling in the years 25 to 5 B.C. from Abusir el Mäläq (τοὺς κατὰ τὸ διάγραμμα τόκους διδράχμους),[83] and recently attested in a contract of money loan for the middle of the second century B.C.[84] No doubt this *diagramma* is of a still earlier origin in the Ptolemaic period.

(7) *Diagramma* on auction sales (διάγραμμα ὠνῆς?), fixing details of a general law concerning sales at auction (νόμος ὠνῆς). It is mentioned in P. Eleph. 14, 27 (= Wilcken, *Chrest.* 340 = Meyer, *Jurist. Papyri* 57). The one detail of the *diagramma* which is preserved fixed the number of days permitted for the offering of land parcels for heritable lease. After the lapse of these days (six days, according to the best reading) the parcel for sale was withdrawn as "unsold" (ἄπρατα). See P. M. Meyer *ad loc.*

[78] P. Rev. 55.1-3.

[79] P. Rev. 103 (broken), line 3: δι]αγράμματι τ[ῶι] ἐκκειμένωι ἐπὶ τῆ[ι ὀ]θο[ν . . . .? See Wilcken, *Gr. Ostraka* I p. 266, for the meaning of βύσσινα ὀθόνια, and cf. *Grundzüge*, I p. 245.

[80] P. Hibeh 116 *recto*, see Introduction, εἰσόδεια τῆς [14 letters?] ἐκ τοῦ ἐπιβάλλοντος [αὐτοῖς (?) κατὰ τὸ δι]άγραμμα ἀν(ὰ) x. Cf. Wilcken, *Gr. Ostraka* I, pp. 264 f.

[81] P. Col. Inv. 270, col. I, 12-13, in *Mem. Am. Acad. in Rome* VI (1927), κατὰ τὸ σιτολογικὸν διάγραμμα.

[82] *Ibid.*, col. III 10-11, καὶ τὴν τιμὴν παντὸς ὑποθεῖναι κατὰ τὸ διάγραμμα τὸ περὶ τῶν σιτικῶν ἐκκείμενον.

[83] B.G.U. IV, see Index under διάγραμμα.

[84] P. Berlin 5883 + 5853, published by Ulrich Wilcken in *Ztsch. für aegypt. Sprache und Altertumskunde*, LX p. 90.

To this list is to be added: (8) the *diagramma* on the slaves, P. Col. Inv. 480.

The wording of P. Paris 62 (= U.P.Z. 112) 5-8 shows that around 200 B.C. there were especial *nomoi, diagrammata, prostagmata* and *diorthomata* upon each type of tax-farming concession.[85] P. Col. Inv. 480 is that part of the *diagramma* on the slaves which determined the incidence and amount of the sale tax on slaves. In the form in which we have it, the *diagramma* was passed before the death of Dicaearchus in 197 B.C. It certainly is not a fundamental ordinance, establishing for the first time the relations of the Ptolemaic state with the slave population of Egypt and the sale tax on slaves. A tax on slave sales, hence also a *diagramma* upon the subject, had existed earlier, in which the one per cent fee on sales of paragraphs 1-3 had gone to Dicaearchus. Under the conditions of this ordinance the clerical fee of paragraphs 4-5 had been substituted as his royal grant. A tax of some kind levied upon slaves had also existed in the time of Philadelphus;[86] and it is to be presumed that the tax on sales of slaves either goes back to the Pharaonic period or was introduced, early in the period of the Greek rule of Egypt, by Cleomenes of Naucratis or by Ptolemy I.

The *diagramma* upon any subject must have been the current form of the ordinance, embodying all changes in details caused by royal decrees and other instructions.

P. GRADENWITZ 1, P. HIBEH 29 AND PS.-ARISTEAS, *ad Philocratem epistula*

The content of the Columbia extract from the *diagramma* on the slaves necessitates a new investigation of the royal decree (*prostagma*) upon slaves, published by Gerhard Plaumann as P. Gradenwitz I,[87] and of P. Hibeh 29. The text of P. Grad. 1, with the addition of a fragment discovered later, as republished by Lewald,[88] reads thus:

βασιλέως πρ]οστάξα[ντος

5 [   ]..λε..ρ( ) α[......]α σῶμα

---

[85] τὰ ὑφ' ἡμῶν διατα(?)]σσόμενα ἐφ' ἐκάστης ὠνῆς according to Wilcken's new reading in U.P.Z. 112.

[86] P. Hibeh 29.

[87] In *Sitz. Heid. Akad., phil.-hist. Kl.*, V (1914), 15 Abh., and a republication of the text, with an additional fragment found in the Frankfort collection, by H. Lewald in *Raccolta Lumbroso*, pp. 340-342.

[88] The readings of lines 4-6, however, are taken from the *editio princeps of* Plaumann, as Lewald did not reproduce them.

[ ]......[......]ν..η.(.?)

[ ]........νων ἀπογραψ[άσ]θω-[89]

σαν] πά[ν]τες πρὸς τὸν ἐπὶ τούτων τε-

ταγμέ[ν]ον παρὰ τοῦ βασιλέως ἀπὸ μηνὸς

10 Γορπια[ίο]υ τοῦ ἐν τῶι ιζ (ἔτει) τοὺς μὲν ἐν Ἀλε-

ξανδρείαι ἔως μηνὸς Δίου τοὺς δ' ἐν

τῆι χώραι ἔως Δύστρου καὶ καταβαλεῖν ἑ-

κάστου τοῦ σώματος (δραχμὰς) κ καὶ εἰς ἀνάλωμα

τῶι πραγματευομένωι δραχμὰς τέσσαρας

15 πλὴν τῶν κ[α]ταβεβληκότων τὴν (ἐξηκονταδραχμίαν) καὶ τὴν

τεσσαρακο[ντ]αδραχμίαν. μὴ ἐξέστω δὲ τῶι

. . . .

"Upon the King's order: Let all those who wish . . . slaves[90] . . . en-
roll before the official designated for these matters by the King, beginning
with the month Gorpiaeus in the seventeenth year, those in Alexandria up
to the month Dius, those in the country up to Dystrus, and pay[91] on each
slave 20 drachmas and for expenses to the official in charge[92] 4 drachmas,
except those who have paid[93] the 60 drachma tax and the 40 drachma tax.
Let it not be possible for the . . ."

The explanations of this difficult text heretofore offered are as follows:

(1)   Plaumann's original conclusion, that it was a decree of the eighteenth
year, either of Ptolemy Philadelphus or of Euergetes I, with the preference for
Philadelphus,[94] establishing for the first time an ownership tax on slaves.

[89] Following Wilcken's reading.   Plaumann and Lewald read ἀπογραψ[άτ]ω[σαν.

[90] Wilcken, in his letter to Plaumann, in P. Grad. 1 pp. 13, 14, would read here αἰ[χ]μάλωτα
σώμα-| [τα, "slaves captured in war," with the additional authority of W. Schubart and
Ibscher. Plaumann is doubtful of the reading, ibid., p. 19.

[91] For the abrupt change from the imperative to accusative-infinitive clause as a frequent
occurrence in the style of laws and decrees, see Plaumann (based on Wilcken), P. Grad. 1,
note to line 12.

[92] In the translation of τῶι πραγματευομένωι I follow Wilcken as against Plaumann.
If otherwise undefined or if not clear by the context ὁ πραγματευόμενος is a general term
applying to any official in the tax farming service. See Grenfell, P. Rev., note to 7, 2. "The
tax farmer" would be τῶι πραγματευομένωι τὴν ὠνήν. Observe that the 4 drachma fee is
actually called the προ-πρατ-ικόν in P. Col. Inv. 480, line 14, which strengthens the case for
τῶι πραγ-ματευομένωι as the person "handling" the affair.

[93] The time indicated by the perfect participle κ[α]ταβεβληκότων is, of course, not absolute,
but relative to that of καταβαλεῖν.

[94] P. Grad. 1, p. 12.

(2)   Wilcken's interesting suggestion, made with distinct reservation,[95] that the *prostagma* was of the eighteenth year of Philadelphus, offering a special sale by the King of war prisoners at Alexandria, the subject of ἀπογραψ[άσ]θωσαν being the intending purchasers, and the purchase price being 20 drachmas.[96]

(3)   Lewald's view, following Gelzer's suggestion in *Berl. phil. Woch.* (1916), p. 10, that it represents a single case of extraordinary taxation on slave owners.[97]

The analogies with the content of P. Col. Inv. 480 are striking, with two differences.   In making the comparison I follow the text of P. Grad. 1 as given in Lewald's reading, without argument upon those points in the interpretations of Plaumann and Wilcken which have been eliminated through the text changes which appear in Lewald's edition, particularly in lines 15-16.

Obviously each of these two papyri deals with a tax upon slaves.   P. Col. Inv. 480 determines the taxes and fees upon sales of slaves.   In the Columbia papyrus the taxes are based throughout on the mina as a unit, implying that the expected price is higher than one mina.   Furthermore, the actual tax, without fees, in most of the cases in P. Col. Inv. 480 ranges around *20 drachmas per mina*—17 5/6 drachmas to the mina in paragraph 1, 20 1/6 drachmas in paragraph 2, 19 drachmas in paragraph 4, 16 5/6 drachmas in paragraph 5. In P. Grad. 1 the taxes were 20 drachmas, 40 drachmas, 60 drachmas— *evidently 20 drachmas per mina* upon slaves of different ages and abilities, which were probably valued at 1 mina, 2 minas, and 3 minas respectively.[98] More striking is the fact that the brokerage fee of P. Col. Inv. 480 (*propoletikon* or *propratikon*) is 4 1/6 drachmas and the "expense" for handling in P. Grad. 1 (εἰς ἀνάλωμα τῶι πραγματευομένωι, lines 13-14) is 4 drachmas. The two marked differences between the two documents are, first,   that

[95] In his letter published in Plaumann's discussion, *ibid.*, pp. 12-15.

[96] Wilcken quotes the interesting propagandist story found in Pseudo-Aristeas, section 22, of an order (*prostagma*) of Philadelphus that all who held Jewish slaves and had carried them into the city (Alexandria) or into the country districts must deliver them up, receiving 20 drachmas per head for them.

[97] *Raccolta Lumbroso*, pp. 341-342.

[98] This observation was made to me, in a slightly different form, by Rostovtzeff when I first consulted him upon the document.   For the necessary difference in price according to technical ability, etc., see Wilcken's letter to Plaumann in *Sitz. Heid. Akad., phil.-hist. Kl.* V p. 12, note 15.

the brokerage fee of 4 drachmas in P. Grad. 1 was remitted in the cases of the 40 drachma and 60 drachma tax payments, that is, upon slaves of the two more expensive classes; and, second, that the fee for handling the sales (the "expense" money of P. Grad. 1) in the one case (P. Col. Inv. 480) goes to the city, in the other (P. Grad. 1) to an especial appointee of the King. In P. Grad. 1 the purchaser, of course, pays all the tax, just as in the sales of P. Col. Inv. 480 which are conducted by the government judiciary and fiscal departments (§§ 3-4). The offer to purchase in P. Grad. 1 was made by declaration on the part of the prospective purchaser. The sale prices being fixed, there was no auction, and no crier's fee ($\kappa\eta\rho\acute{\upsilon}\kappa\epsilon\iota o\nu$) appears.

Even the 20 drachma payment of P. Gradenwitz 1 is too high for an *annual* ownership tax, seeing that the earning capacity of unskilled farm labor in the time of Philadelphus, whether free or slave, was about an obol a day, *i.e.*, about 60 drachmas a year, if one figures upon but five holidays.[99] It is probably due to this consideration that Gelzer and Lewald adopted the theory of a *special* tax on slave owners to explain the document. On the basis of its similarities with P. Col. Inv. 480, cited above, it is my conclusion that P. Grad. 1 also is to be interpreted as the application of a sale tax upon slaves which the Ptolemaic government was selling, as a "job lot," at 1 mina. In my interpretation it is necessary to assume that the slaves valued at 2 minas or 3 minas were being disposed of under a separate government sale (note the use of the perfect tense, $\kappa\alpha\tau\alpha\beta\epsilon\beta\lambda\eta\kappa\acute{o}\tau\omega\nu$, in line 15) which was to precede the sale of the 1 mina slaves, and that any person purchasing a 1 mina slave who had previously purchased one of the higher priced slaves and paid his 40 drachma or 60 drachma sale tax was to be exempted from the 4 drachma "expense" fee upon any 1 mina slave which he might purchase.[100] I do not believe that the remission can be understood as applying to the 20 drachma tax as well as to the expense fee of 4 drachmas. With the acceptance of these changes, necessitated in part by H. Lewald's new readings (the $\dot{\epsilon}\xi\eta\kappa o\nu\tau\alpha\delta\rho\alpha\chi\mu\acute{\iota}\alpha\nu$ and $\tau\epsilon\sigma\sigma\alpha\rho\alpha\kappa o[\nu\tau]\alpha\delta\rho\alpha\chi\mu\acute{\iota}\alpha\nu$), Ulrich Wilcken's discussion of the text offers a rational and attractive theory in explanation of

[99] A twenty per cent ownership tax applied annually would mean that the taxes paid would equal the original purchase price of a slave in five years.

[100] P. Grad. 1, 12-16. The purchasers shall pay the 20 drachma fee and a 4 drachma expense fee, $\pi\lambda\grave{\eta}\nu$ $\tau\hat{\omega}\nu$ $\kappa[\alpha]\tau\alpha\beta\epsilon\beta\lambda\eta\kappa\acute{o}\tau\omega\nu$ $\tau\grave{\eta}\nu$ $(\dot{\epsilon}\xi\eta\kappa o\nu\tau\alpha\delta\rho\alpha\chi\mu\acute{\iota}\alpha\nu)$ $\kappa\alpha\grave{\iota}$ $\tau\grave{\eta}\nu$ $\tau\epsilon\sigma\sigma\alpha\rho\alpha\kappa o[\nu\tau]\alpha\delta\rho\alpha\mu\chi\acute{\iota}\alpha\nu$.

the large number of slaves which the Ptolemaic state had to sell at this time and of the unusual methods of the sale.

Starting with the known factor of the sale tax on slaves in Egypt about 200 B.C., the probability is great that this tax goes back to the earliest period of the Greek occupation. Whether it was introduced under Cleomenes of Naucratis or early in the rule of Soter, as a source of revenue new to Egypt, we can not know. Our knowledge of the tax systems of the Greek states, and especially of the slave tax, is very limited; but that a tax on slave sales existed in the sixth century in Cyzicus is certain.[101] The "tax upon the slaves" at Athens mentioned by Xenophon[102] has generally been regarded as an ownership tax; but it may equally well be explained as a tax on sales.[103] There is, therefore, no existing document, so far as my knowledge goes,[104] which really proves an ownership tax on slaves either in Ptolemaic Egypt or in the earlier Greek city-state organizations.

Assuming that the tax on slave sales existed in the time of Philadelphus, neither the style[105] nor the arrangements for the sales depicted in P. Grad. 1 conform to the *customary* method of slave sales and the application of this tax as shown by P. Col. Inv. 480. Instead of the customary officials connected with sales a special appointee of the King appears (τὸν ἐπὶ τούτων τεταγμένον παρὰ τοῦ βασιλέως). There is a set time limit within which the purchasers may announce themselves: seven months for those from the countryside, three months for those in Alexandria. The entire sale is set for Alexandria. Instead of the *propoletikon*, or brokerage fee, which appears in the private sales of P. Col. Inv. 480 (paragraphs 1-3) and is paid to the city, we find a fee of similar amount (4 drachmas as against 4 1/6 drachmas) which was to be paid to the special commissioner appointed by the King—and it is called by the untechnical term of "expense fee," corresponding to the usage of ἀνάλωμα so common in private accounts. In other words, this trans-

---

[101] The ἀνδραποδωνίη of Ditt. *Syll.*³ I 4.

[102] Xenophon, *Oec.* 4, 25: ὅσον τὸ τέλος τῶν ἀνδραπόδων πρὸ τῶν ἐν Δεκελεία.

[103] Despite the argument of Fränkel in Boeckh, *Staatshaushaltung der Athener* (2d edition), note 546, in Vol. II, *Anm.*, p. 79.

[104] Cf. the statement of the editors of P. Hibeh 29, Introduction, on the information as it stood in 1906 in regard to a general slave tax. I cannot accept P. Hibeh 29 as proving the existence of an ownership tax on slaves.

[105] See Wilcken's remarks upon the aorists in P. Grad. 1, lines 7, 12, in his letter to Plaumann, p. 12. Cf. Mayser, *Grammatik* II p. 150 § 36, b, 1.

action has the appearance of being one carried on by the King as representing the royal *oikos*. For this reason Wilcken's reading of αἰ[χ]μάλωτα σώμα-|τα in line 5 is particularly attractive. Even without the support of this reading the document indicates that in the year 17 of his reign Ptolemy Philadelphus (or Ptolemy Euergetes?) came into possession of a large number of slaves, and that these were announced by special decree for sale at Alexandria, allowing for a prolonged period for registration, by intending purchasers, of their names. If this general conclusion is accepted it is possible to assume that in the regular system of sales of slaves of the time of Ptolemy II or Ptolemy III, as expressed in the διάγραμμα τῶν ἀνδραπόδων of the time of P. Grad. 1, the sale tax was arbitrarily fixed at 20 drachmas, 40 drachmas, 60 drachmas respectively[106] per slave sold, instead of at a true percentage *ad valorem* such as appears in the later ordinance preserved in P. Col. Inv. 480.

P. Hibeh 29, *recto* (= Wilcken, *Chrest.* 259), of about 265 B.C., was regarded by the editors as a royal ordinance upon the farming of a tax on slaves, leaving the question in doubt as to whether they considered it to be a sale tax or a special tax upon ownership.[107] Since its publication it has sometimes been regarded as part of a law (νόμος τελωνικός) regulating the farming of a property tax on slaves.[108] To the interpretation of this document P. Col. Inv. 480 brings only the one addition, but a fundamental one, that a tax on transfers of slaves is attested for the late third century B.C.,[109] with the great probability that it had existed from the earliest period of Ptolemaic rule. Four points in P. Hibeh 29 speak for its content as applying to the farming of the sale tax on slaves:[110]—first, the implication in lines 5-6 (πραθέ[ντος] τοῦ ἀνδραπόδου) that the slave had been destined for sale; second, the fact

---

[106] Note τὴν ἑξηκονταδραχμίαν καὶ τὴν τεσσαρακο[ντ]αδραχμίαν of P. Grad. 1, 15, 16.
[107] See P. Hib. 29, Introduction.
[108] As in Wilcken, *Grundzüge der Papyrusk.* I, 1, p. 171, where it appears among the "*Vermögenssteuer*," and in *Chrestomathie* I.2, 259 Introduction (*Sklavenbesitzer*).
[109] As I am informed by A. S. Hunt, who kindly checked the point by rereading P. Hib. 29 at my request, in line 2 ἀλλαξ[άμενος σῶμ]α ὑ[πόχρ]εον (cf. the ὑποχρέων σωμάτων of P. Col. Inv. 480, 18), though it fits the space, would be a doubtful restoration. He writes: "If the letter before the bracket is υ (which is far from certain) I can't reconcile the preceding remains with α. Moreover, I much doubt if the letter before ν was ο, since there is an appearance of the remains of a linking stroke which would suit *e.g.* α or ε, but not ο or ι."
[110] For a contemporary use of ὑποτιθέναι in the sense of pledging a person, see P.S.I. IV 424, 10-15. The question of the slave as pledged object would play no part if it were an ownership tax.

that the slaves dealt with, certainly in one of the sections of the document, possibly in all of them, were mortgaged slaves (ἐὰν δὲ ὁ ὑπ[οτε]θεὶς μηνύσηι, line 7);[111] third, the connection of the operations of P. Hibeh 29 with the offices of the *agoranomi* which is attested for the slave sales in P. Col. Inv. 480;[112] and fourth, the publishing by the tax farmer of a list, το[ῦτο τὸ] γραμματ-[εῖον],[113] of the cases under discussion (the mortgages), this list to be made up by the secretary on the slaves, the checking clerk and the tax farmer. If the document dealt with an ownership tax the necessity of publishing such a list would be incomprehensible to me. The primary subject of P. Hibeh 29 *recto*, so far as preserved, seems to be the establishment of procedure and penalties for infraction of the laws and for failure to do their duty, affecting both the officials in charge of the sales and the vendors of a certain type of slave (ὁ ὑπ[οτε]θεὶς, line 6; the possible ὑ[ποτεθ]έν in line 2; τὰς ὑποθέσεις, line 7).

The assumption has been made that the taxes and fees upon manumissions as fixed for the tax farmers would be found in the Columbia *diagramma* if we had it in complete form. The same supposition may also be made for the emancipation tax established by the editors of P. Hibeh 29.[114] The Pseudo-Aristeas letter to Philocrates, to which Wilcken called attention in his discussion of P. Gradenwitz 1, contains an alleged decree of Ptolemy Philadelphus by which over a hundred thousand Jews were emancipated who were then in servitude in Egypt. This alleged *prostagma* of the King made mandatory upon their owners the declaration (by *apographe*) of all Jewish slaves then held in slavery in Egypt, within three days after publication of the decree (§24). The declarations were to be made to the regular magistrates and the slaves delivered to these magistrates. Punishment of confiscation of property

[111] Cf. Schönbauer, *Liegenschaftsrecht*, p. 30, who acutely recognized the *agoranomi* in P. Hibeh 29 as the magistrates entrusted with the official recording in the case of mortgaged slaves.

[112] ἐπὶ τῶν ἀγορανόμων in line 4.

[113] The reading τὸ [διά]γραμμα τ[όδε] proposed by A. Wilhelm in *Beiträge zur greichischen Inschriftenkunde*, p. 247 (inaccessible to me; but see Wilcken, *Papyrusk. Chrestomathie* 259, note to line 9) would make the entire recto of P. Hib. 29 a *diagramma*. The restoration is made questionable by the serious doubt whether a tax farmer would be entrusted with the publishing of a royal ordinance, and by the content, which does not deal solely with the subject of a *diagramma* of the judicial type, nor with that of a *diagramma* which determines and readjusts detailed prices, conversion values, taxes and the like.

[114] See their note to line 7.

was decreed for anyone who disobeyed the law, on the condition that proven owners of slaves alone were to be held liable.[115] Those who freed their Jewish slaves were to receive forthwith 20 drachmas upon each slave, the soldiers at the time of receiving their pay, civilians at the royal bank (§22).

The Pseudo-Aristeas letter is a panegyric upon Jewish wisdom and upon the Jewish Law. Its date of composition is placed by Schürer about 200 B.C.,[116] by Paul Wendland in the later Maccabean period, between 130 and 62 B.C.[117] The incident of the emancipation of the Jewish slaves and the fictitious *prostagma* of Philadelphus, if this also is to be considered a forgery, were nevertheless written with some knowledge of the Ptolemaic law upon slavery and of the forms of such decrees. In the Aristeas letter the alleged decree of Ptolemy II is presented as an emancipation act by royal *fiat*. The 20 drachma payment established by King Ptolemy must, also, be regarded as having a basis of historical actuality.[118] As presented in the *prostagma* it is a flat rate which is made to the holders of all slaves, without reference to their values as determined by age or by physical and technical qualifications, applying to newborn children still at the breast (§27) or to mature slaves. For this reason, even considering the fact that the action of the Ptolemaic government was alleged to have affected over a hundred thousand Jews, it does not seem possible to regard the 20 drachma payment as a purchase price. In consideration of the new information gleaned from P. Col. Inv. 480 in combination with P. Hibeh 29, the following explanation of the 20 drachma rate is presented as more feasible than its interpretation as an actual purchase price.[119] The writer of the *epistula* conceived it as a small compensation to the dispossessed slave owners, a concession made by the government to the former owners in consideration of a very considerable financial loss. Its amount, the round number of 20 drachmas, may have been sug-

---

[115] §25. This seems to be a provision designed to protect innocent persons against false informers.

[116] *Geschichte des jüdischen Volkes*, 3d ed., III, pp. 466-470.

[117] P. Wendland, *Aristeae ad Philocratem Epistula*, Leipzig, 1900, XXVII.

[118] Cf. Ulrich Wilcken, ὑπομνηματισμοί, in *Philologus* 53 (1894), p. 111.

[119] In *Ps.-Aristeas ep.* § 37, edition of Wendland, I interpret ἀποδόντες τοῖς κρατοῦσι τὴν κατ' ἀξίαν ἀργυρικὴν τιμήν to mean: "paying to the owners the price (the fixed payment of 20 drachmas) on the silver standard, according to ratio," *i.e.*, according to the ratio of copper to silver as fixed in the existing *diagramma* upon that subject.

gested by the customary sale tax upon slaves of cheaper valuation, as in P. Gradenwitz 1, or possibly by the amount of the tax imposed by the government upon slaves freed by the process of emancipation.[120]

THE TAX UPON SLAVE SALES AND THE FEES

In terminology there is no fundamental distinction made in the Ptolemaic tax legislation as represented in P. Col. Inv. 480—though there is in the accounting system—between the actual tax and the fees or subsidiary charges, such as would indicate an approach toward a scientific analysis of taxation methods. The tendency is to regard them all under the comprehensive classification "all the taxes."[121] The bookkeeping requirements of the fiscal department, by the necessity of separate allocation to a specific chest (fiscal purpose) or by shifting the incidence of a particular fee upon buyer or seller, made continued separation of fees and the tax a practical need. This may be illustrated, in the paragraphs covering private sales, by the inclusion among the taxes ($\tau\grave{\alpha}$ $\tau\acute{\epsilon}\lambda\eta$ $\pi\acute{\alpha}\nu\tau\alpha$, paragraph 2, line 11) of the *hekatoste* (one per cent fee) which had formerly been collected for the grant to Dicaearchus, and its inclusion with the portion of the tax falling upon the vendor.[122] The fee for handling (the *propoletikon* or *propratikon*), in the same cases of sales between individuals, is constantly spoken of separately because of its allocation to the city of Alexandria. In the compulsory sales by auction through the judicial and fiscal departments (paragraphs 4-5), the herald's fee and the clerical fee are maintained as separate entities because of their separate assignment, in the one case as the emolument of the crier's service, in the other as the grant to Dicaearchus.

Though the incidence of the tax varies, a distinct tendency is noticeable. In paragraph 1, in which the method was that of a definite agreement between buyer and seller with registration of the sale before the market supervisors, more than a half of the taxes and fees fell upon the vendor. This has been explained, in the separate discussion of the paragraph, by reference to the advantages which this method of sale offered to the vendor and the government—to the vendor by acceptance of a price satisfactory to him; to

---

[120] As in P. Hibeh 29, 7. See note of the editors.

[121] P. Col. Inv. 480, 7. Customs duties were called $\tau\acute{\epsilon}\lambda\eta$, *e.g.*, P. Rev. 52, 18, 21, 23, and tolls likewise, P. Cairo Zenon I 59060, 10; 59061, 5; II 59240, 7.

[122] P. Col. Inv. 480, paragraph 1, lines 6-8.

the state by greater simplicity of operation in the conduct of the sale. The shifting of this part of the tax from buyer to seller looks, therefore, like a justified concession to that party in the transaction who otherwise derived no advantage from this form of sale. Paragraphs 2 and 3 have been explained as voluntary, or private, sales in which the government's auctioning system has been resorted to, paragraph 2 dealing with primary bids which were accepted by the seller, paragraph 3 with those cases in which a secondary bidding and a third bid (counterbid) occurred. For the sales by the government officials (the *praktor xenikon* and the officials of the finance department respectively, in sections 4 and 5) the incidence of the tax and fees must necessarily have been upon the purchaser. In the case of the payment of debts which had resulted in the submission of the debtor's person to the creditor, the creditor is responsible for only one half of the taxes, the debtor for the other half and the clerical fee. In this case the creditor corresponded to the purchaser. The debtor corresponded to the vendor, as the one who transferred his own physical or mental services to the creditor. The general tendency noticeable throughout the document is, therefore, that the sale taxes rested upon the purchaser. This tendency may best be explained on purely empirical grounds and ascribed to the observation of ancient tax legislators that the purchaser customarily had the money and that the easiest administration of the tax lay in obtaining it from him.[123]

The practice of exacting the tax on sales from the purchaser is, with one exception, completely borne out by the history of the various types of the ἐγκύκλιον taxes,[124] including those upon sales of land, sales of houses, and the sales of the priestly emoluments connected with the cult of the dead, which came in upon festival days at the various temples (the ἀγνευτικαὶ ἡμέραι).[125] The sole divergence from this rule which has come to my notice is that of the

[123] It would be unwarranted, of course, to ascribe to the ancient tax legislators any of the modern ideas of taxation theory, such as the theory of "ability to pay" in this instance. Partsch had long since noted, in the extant examples of the sale tax on slaves from the Roman period, that the acquirer (purchaser) paid the tax; *Sitz. Heid. Akad., phil.-hist. Kl.* VII, Abh. 10, p. 26. No doubt this was only a tendency, as in the Ptolemaic period.

[124] See the references and discussions in Wilcken, *Ostraka,* I pp. 182-185, introduction to P. Teb. II 350, and notably Wilcken's penetrating observations in U.P.Z. I p. 511. The rule and the exception have been noted by Wilcken, *ibid.,* p. 183, note 3. Upon gifts of similar properties the recipient pays the tax (Ptolemaic example, B.G.U. 993; Roman, P. Teb. II 351).

[125] See Otto, *Priester und Tempel* II pp. 31-32, 175 n. 2, and Wilcken, *Archiv* IX (1928), pp. 76-77.

London bilingual receipt long since published by Revillout,[126] in which the tax is divided between buyer and seller, as in the slave sale tax of P. Col. Inv. 480 under the conditions of its paragraph 1. In addition to this outstanding peculiarity the London bilingual receipt (for the ἐγκύκλιον on a sale of land) is distinguished by the unusual amount of the tax. The ἐγκύκλιον tax, in the extant examples, had previously been at a fixed rate of five per cent in 228-227 B.C.;[127] and it continued at this rate in examples of 162 B.C. and 139 B.C.[128] Sometime between 139 B.C. and the years 126 and 125 B.C. the ἐγκύκλιον tax had been raised to ten per cent (διδραχμία τῶν κ′ ἡ ἔστιν δεκάτη).[129] In the London bilingual receipt (Preisigke, Sammelbuch 5729) the ἐγκύκλιον stands at the peculiar figure of 8 drachmas 2 1/4 obols (to the mina), meaning eight per cent plus. This rate is also found in P. Lond. 1200,[130] which seems to have been dated with certainty by Wilcken as of the fourteenth year of Ptolemy Philopator,[131] or 208 B.C. On the analogy with P. Col. Inv. 480 and the close relation necessarily existing between its slave sale tax and the real property tax represented by the *enkyklion*, I offer the following tentative proposal in explanation of the variations in the *enkyklion* rate:

(1) Somewhere between 227 and 209 B.C. the system and the rate of the *enkyklion* was changed so that 8 drachmas 2 1/4 obols to the mina (eight per cent plus) might be the exaction on certain types of the sales. I doubt that

---

[126] In *Proceed. Soc. Bibl. Arch.* XIV (1892), pp. 120-132. Republished by Preisigke, *Sammelbuch* 5729.

[127] P. Hibeh 70, a and b.

[128] See P.S.I. VIII 1014 for the five per cent ἐγκύκλιον in 171 B.C.; B.G.U. 992 and P. Ryl. 248 for the same rate in 162 B.C., and P. Amh. 52 for 139 B.C. Add P.S.I. VIII 1015, of 142 B.C., which records payment of the five per cent sale tax, (εἰκοστή) τοῦ εγκυ(κλίου), on the transfer of a house and of ἀγνευτικαὶ ἡμέραι. Both of these sales were obviously taxed at the same five per cent rate.

[129] P. Teb. II 280 and 281. Four new examples of the ten per cent sales tax on real property were added by Preisigke, P. Strassburg 82 (115 B.C.), 84 (114 B.C.), 86 (111 B.C.), and 87 (107 B.C.), three of the same period in P. Ryl. 249-251, of 118, 117 and 113 B.C.; and one, dated 115 B.C., in P.S.I. VIII 1017. The ten per cent tax which appears in Viereck, *Griechische und demotische Ostraka*, the demotic subscription to no. 35, does not fit into this scheme and should not be identified with the *enkyklion*, because it is paid in two successive years.

[130] P. Lond. III pp. 2-3.

[131] On the ground that it comes from Thebes and that the Thebaid was reconquered only in the nineteenth year of Ptolemy V. See U.P.Z. I p. 511. The relation of the ἐγκύκλιον rate of 8 drachmas 2 1/4 obols to that in Preisigke, *Sammelbuch* 5729, and now to the rate of the taxes on slaves in P. Col. Inv. 480, gives strong support to Wilcken's dating.

the close correspondence of this rate with the 8 drachmas 2 1/2 obols tax per mina exacted from the seller of a slave under the conditions of P. Col. Inv. 480, paragraph 1, can be regarded as implying any direct connection between the two forms of taxes.

(2)   In the revision of the law which brought about this change,[132] provision was made that under certain conditions (unknown to us) a part of this *enkyklion* would be shifted to the vendor,[133] corresponding to the methods of incidence of the slave sale tax of that time.   This is contrary to the previous and to the later tendency of the *enkyklion* as applied in Egypt, where the purchaser customarily paid the entire tax.   From a statement of Tacitus it is clear that the slave sale tax imposed at Rome was levied in the same way, *i.e.*, upon the purchasers, up to 56 A.D.   An attempt made by Nero's advisers in that year to shift the tax to the vendors was unsuccessful in attaining the end desired, according to Tacitus, because the dealers shifted it again, by increasing the price, to the buyers.[134]

(3)   There is a large probability that the change made in the revision of this tax permitted the exaction of different *ad valorem* rates corresponding to different methods of sale.   Some arrangement of this type, suggested by the analogy of P. Col. Inv. 480, would allow for the appearance of the five per cent *ad valorem* rate in P. Petr. III 57b, dated in 201 B.C.[135]   The receipt for

---

[132] τὸ ἐκκείμενον πρόσταγμα of P. Lond. III 1200 (p. 12), line 8.   Cf. Wilcken's acute suggestion to this effect in U.P.Z. I p. 511, note 2.

[133] Preisigke, *Sammelbuch* 5729, of 209 B.C.   But the purchaser alone pays the whole amount in P. Lond. III 1200 (pp. 2-3), corresponding probably to the arrangement made possible in P. Col. Inv. 480, paragraph 2.

[134] Tacitus, *Annals* XIII 31, *quia cum venditor pendere iuberetur, in partem pretii emptoribus adcrescebat.*   Actually the incidence of the sale taxes probably was upon buyer and seller, in changing degrees, whoever paid it.   I judge that the statement of Tacitus can only be interpreted as meaning that the government thought that it could meet some sort of complaint as to the slave sale tax by collecting it from the seller; that this did not affect the situation as desired; possibly that it did not work out well from the standpoint of the administration of the tax.   The implication is that the Roman state returned later to the old system.

[135] The assumption of Wilcken, U.P.Z. I p. 511, 516, that the ἐγκύκλιον of P. Paris 62 (=U.P.Z. I 112) VI, 7 is the same as the ἐπιδέκατον, that is, "the excess ten per cent," of that same document, col. I 15, and the results deduced from that assumption, are complicated and difficult for me to follow.   Apart from this assumption (ἐγκύκλιον = ἐπιδέκατον of col. I 15) the statement would mean that the right was permitted to tax farmers who have the concession for several taxes in the same year, to assign excesses of one concession against deficits in another, *except for the "enkyklion," or sale tax.*   This was Wilcken's original viewpoint; see U.P.Z. I p. 516, note 5.

the (δεκάτη) ἐγκυ(κλίου), or ten per cent sale tax, appended to B.G.U. 999, of 99 B.C., gives only 100 drachmas as tax payment on a sale amounting to 2000 drachmas, which is only five per cent. The possibility, seen in P. Col. Inv. 480, of shifting a part of the tax from purchaser to vendor may now be used to explain the discrepancy between the ten per cent tax and the five per cent payment here recorded, in preference to the assumption of an error in the recorded payment of 100 drachmas instead of 200 drachmas.[136]

The ten per cent *enkyklion* rate on real property sales was maintained through the first two centuries of the Roman rule.[137] Ostraka appear in the second century in which the designation of the slave sale tax (as an *enkyklion*) has been assimilated to that of the sale tax on real property as the τέλος ἐνκυκ(λίου) ἀνδραπ(όδων);[138] but its amount is unknown.

To the history of the *kerykeion*, or herald's fee, the testimony of P. Col. Inv. 480 adds nothing new. Throughout the Columbia document I have identified the one per cent fee (*hekatoste*) as the charge for herald's services, whether specifically so designated by addition of *kerykeion* or not. In paragraphs 2 and 3, where auction by the state auctioning organization certainly occurred, the herald's fee is included in the gross tax and fees, fixed at 20 drachmas 1 obol. The only type of transfer recorded in the *diagramma* in which the herald's fee does not appear is that of paragraph 6, on the self-submission of bonded debtors. The explanation of this fact probably lies in the obvious desire to make the tax burden as light as possible upon this form of transference of one's personal services, in the interest of the debtor. It is also clear that no auction actually takes place in such cases. But this was equally true in the case of the transfers with *katagraphe* of paragraph 1, where the one per cent fee was nevertheless applied. But the motive of the greatest possible reduction of the tax burden does not apply in the transfers of paragraph 1. The herald's fee would, therefore, be exacted on such transfers, as a regular charge customarily attached to all slave sales. The omission of the designation *kerykeion*, as herald's fee, may possibly find its explanation in the fact that the process of auction does not, in reality, take place. The

---

[136] See the statement of the editors of P. Teb. II 350, Introduction.
[137] P. Teb. II 350, Introduction; P. Oxy. X 1284, Introduction.
[138] Wilcken, *Ostraka* II 1454; cf. 1066.

charge for crier's service on the sale of slaves about 200 B.C. stood at one per cent, which is the rate found in the compulsory auction of land by the state in the Zois papyri of 158-148 B.C.[139] As in its previous appearances, the herald's fee is charged on all sales of goods by auction which were conducted by the state.[140] Ordinary sales of *mobilia* were not under the strict government control evidenced for sales of real estate and slaves. In case of a sale of *mobilia*, therefore, if the seller wished to advertise a forthcoming sale, he might hire a herald, possibly the community herald, but at his own expense.[141] As compared with the brokerage fee ($\pi\rho\sigma\pi\omega\lambda\eta\tau\iota\kappa\acute{o}\nu$, $\pi\rho\sigma\pi\rho\alpha\tau\iota\kappa\acute{o}\nu$) and the clerical fee (*graphion*), the herald's fee has the marked peculiarity that it is an *ad valorem* charge. The specific charge, such as that of 4 1/6 drachmas per slave for handling and 1 drachma per slave for clerical work, seems the more rational method, in that the difficulty of conducting the sale and recording its various operations is no greater in the case of a high-priced slave than in that of a low-priced one.[142]

The $\pi\rho\sigma\pi\omega\lambda\eta\tau\iota\kappa\acute{o}\nu$ of P. Col. Inv. 480, 10 and the $\pi\rho\sigma\pi\rho\alpha\tau\iota\kappa\acute{o}\nu$ of line 14 are the same fee, a specific charge of 4 drachmas 1 obol per slave sold, irrespective of the value involved in the transfer. In case the slave is sold by higher bid it is exacted twice, if by counterbid ($\dot{\alpha}\nu\theta\upsilon\pi\epsilon\rho\beta\sigma\lambda\acute{\eta}$) three times (paragraph 3), from the purchaser. This requirement emphasizes the fee as a charge for service rendered and necessarily repeated in the case of an overbid and a counterbid. The only other appearance of the $\pi\rho\sigma\pi\omega\lambda\eta\tau\iota\kappa\acute{o}\nu$ known to me is that in P. Rev. 55, 15, in a marginal correction dealing with the wages paid to the workers in the oil monopoly and the pay of the tax farmers. In the sales of slaves of P. Col. Inv. 480 the brokerage fee *is paid to the city of*

---

[139] U.P.Z. I 114. See Wilcken's discussion in note to line 4. Cf. P. Eleph. 14, 12, auctioning of heritable lease in which it stands at one one-thousandth, or one-tenth of the rate in P. Col. Inv. 480 and P. Zois.

[140] For the Roman period, see the sales of monopolies and other public sales in P. Fay. 36, 16-18; B.G.U. VI 1218, 1221, 1222; P. Ryl. 215, lines 44, 51 and Introduction.

[141] Cf. Vitelli's note to P.S.I. V 543, 59 (a Zenon papyrus) on the *kerykeion* on a private sale of two donkeys. J. Partsch in *Archiv* V p. 501 has explained the legal implications of the use of the herald in state sales. The persons who may have any legal right in the object auctioned by the state lose this right by silence against the bids, the heralding of the sale being the required publicity for it. The economic reason, that of advertising the sale, was no doubt the primary one in the use of the crier.

[142] The charge for "expense" ($\dot{\alpha}\nu\acute{\alpha}\lambda\omega\mu\alpha$) in P. Grad. 1, 14 is also a specific charge of 4 drachmas per slave sold.

Alexandria; and it appears only in the sales executed between private individuals (paragraphs 1-3). Where it appears no clerical fee (*graphion*) is charged.

In the approach to the problem of the payment of the brokerage fee to the city of Alexandria, the general application of the *diagrammata* as legislation precludes the explanation that we are here dealing with a mere extract from the city laws which would apply to the city alone, without any application to the kingdom of Egypt as a whole. In explanation of the payment of the brokerage fee to the city two possibilities present themselves. The first is that in the voluntary transfers of slaves between private parties (paragraphs 1-3), the slave market was confined to the city of Alexandria. The observation that in P. Gradenwitz 1 the *apographai* of prospective purchasers of slaves are to be sent in to a single personage appointed by the King, who was evidently located in the city,[143] seems to commend this conclusion. Under this explanation the transfers made between individuals, without compulsion and with *katagraphe* before the market supervisors, did not actually require an auction sale or the appearance of the slave in person in the slave market. In such cases the business of transfer could be conducted in any part of Egypt and the brokerage fee could be collected by the local tax farmers and placed upon their records as allocated to the city of Alexandria. But the auction sales of paragraphs 2-3, if we confine the slave market to Alexandria, would have to take place in the city. This seems incredible because of the great cost and inconvenience of shipping slaves out of all parts of the *chora* to Alexandria which would be necessary. Such a requirement would have the effect of eliminating most of such transfers between private persons living in the *chora* when the sales were conducted by use of the government auctioning machinery.

The second explanation of the *propoletikon* seems much more probable. The original Ptolemaic *diagramma* on the slaves and slave-selling may have been modeled upon the Greek city laws of Alexandria (as proposed by Rostovtzeff in the *Cambridge Ancient History*, VII p. 895), wherein the city re-

---

[143] As indicated by the special arrangement for an additional four months for the registration of names of purchasers from the *chora* as against those living in Alexandria. In P. Grad. 1 the *analoma*, or fee for expenses, corresponds to the *propoletikon* of P. Col. Inv. 480, except that in P. Grad. 1 it goes to the special appointee of the King who managed the sale.

ceived a brokerage fee for handling all slave sales in the city. The city's fee may have gone over into the general *diagramma* upon the subject for entire Egypt when this original *diagramma* was first formulated. In that case the *propoletikon* had become, in effect, a *dorea* applied throughout Egypt for the maintenance of the city which was the capital of Egypt and the seat of the royal residence.

THE DEBTOR SLAVES (*Hypochrea Somata*)

Although the necessity of comparing the status of the ὑπόχρεον σῶμα with that of the Roman *nexus* immediately suggests itself, the better approach to its understanding is from our knowledge of the earlier Greek practices of debtor bondage. The material upon the Greek practice has been gathered and discussed, with emphasis from the juristic standpoint, by Heinrich Swoboda.[144] In pre-Solonian Athens execution upon the person and slavery for debt *through judgment* was applied to citizens.[145] Contractual enslavement for debt, *i.e.*, without judgment, is proven for the Greek law of Crete in the Second Law of Gortyn.[146] The debtor mortgaged his own person, and, upon non-fulfillment of his liability, entered into a status of quasi-slavery, with diminution of his personal rights so long as his condition of debtor bondage persisted. During this period he was called ὁ κατακείμενος.[147] According to the wording of the law he was regarded as unfree during the continuation of this status.[148] The Lygdamis inscription of Halicarnassus (about 454 B.C.) proves that citizens of Halicarnassus might be condemned to sale into slavery in foreign parts for attempting to abrogate the law upon the conduct of cases dealing with house property and land.[149] There is an important restriction upon this right of sale into slavery in that it applies only to those whose property was valued at less than 10 staters. For citizens of higher financial

---

[144] Über die altgriechische Schuldknechtschaft," in *Sav.-Ztsch.* XXVI (1905), *Röm. Abt.*, pp. 190-280.

[145] For the correction of Swoboda's view (*loc. cit.*, p. 213) that Solon's words are a proof of voluntary self-submission of the debtor to bondage, see *Dikaiomata*, p. 123.

[146] Collitz, *Gr. Dialektinschr.* 3², 4998.

[147] Swoboda, *Sav.-Ztsch.* XXVI p. 196.

[148] See the law in Swoboda, *loc. cit.*, pp. 145-195, col. VI: ὁ καταθέμενος μωλησετῖ καὶ πραχσῆται τὰς τιμάνς (for the debtor slave) ἀι ἐλευθέρω (ἀι = ὡς, see Blass, *Rh. Mus.* XLI, p. 314). Swoboda on the basis of this passage came to the opposite conclusion that the κατακείμενος was free, *loc. cit.*, p. 196.

[149] Dittenberger, *Sylloge³* 45, 31-35.

rating the punishment was confiscation of property and perpetual banishment. How far such restriction upon enslavement of citizens extended generally in the laws of the other Greek states remains doubtful.[150] At least we have the proof in the law of Gortyn of an early Greek practice of self-mortgage and self-submission to bondage in case of non-payment, corresponding in its general features to the *nexum* relationship of Roman citizens before the passage of the *lex Poetelia*. We have also the proof of a restricted application, as a penal measure, of sale into slavery outside the bounds of the state. For non-citizen classes, we must assume that the possibilities both of voluntary pledge of the person for debt, with the consequences of conditional bondage, and of ultimate complete slavery for debt, were much greater, and their application much more frequent.

In the case of Egypt Diodorus Siculus is authority for the knowledge[151] that enslavement of debtors in case of non-payment, which had been recognized in the law of Pharaonic Egypt, was abolished by decree of Bocchoris (Pharoah Bakenranef, about 718-712 B.C.).[152] It has long been known that the practice of mortgaging the person on the part of debtors and enslavement for non-payment was permitted in Ptolemaic times;[153] but the reservation has commonly been made that such action was largely fiscal, and doubt has been expressed that execution upon the person of debtors actually led to slavery.[154] There is no evidence known to me telling when or how the law of Bocchoris became inactive, whether by a gradual process of nullification by disuse or by a special law which repealed it. P. Hibeh 88 and 92 brought the information that the right of execution upon the person had been regulated in a Ptolemaic *diagramma* promulgated before 262 B.C.[155] P. Halensis 1, dated by the editors as of the end of the reign of Ptolemy II or of the early years of Ptolemy III, added the knowledge that citizens of Alexandria might be enslaved, but not

[150] See *Dikaiomata*, p. 81.

[151] Diodorus Siculus I 79.

[152] It did appear, however, in the sixth century under Amasis II: *cf.* F. Ll. Griffith, *Demotic Papyri in the John Rylands Library*, III (1909) p. 51.

[153] L. Wenger, *Archiv für Papyrusforschung* II, p. 53.

[154] Mitteis, *Grundzüge*, II 1, p. 20. Bouché-Leclercq, *Histoire des Lagids* IV p. 119, considered such action rare and merely provisional when it was applied.

[155] H. Lewald, *Zur Personalexekution*, p. 31. For actual cases of imprisonment for debt see P.S.I. 529 (the debtor himself under arrest) and P.S.I. 532 (sons of a debtor under arrest for debt).

to fellow citizens.[156]   The passage obviously includes slavery resulting from debt, though other causes of slavery may be contemplated.   The editors have rightly drawn the conclusion that this paragraph of the city law implies that no Alexandrian citizen, male or female, might be enslaved to any person, whether Egyptian subject or Alexandrian citizen, *within the city territory.*[157] Sale of Alexandrian citizens to non-citizens resident in Alexandria, that is, to foreigners and to Egyptian subjects in the city, certainly was not contemplated in the law.   The necessary deduction is that even Alexandrian citizens were subject to execution upon the person for debt and eventual sale into foreign lands or to persons who were not fellow citizens in case such persons were resident elsewhere in Egypt.

To this body of information upon debtor slavery now comes the evidence contained in the Columbia *diagramma*, paragraphs 5 and 6.   It leaves no doubt that the practice was commonly enforced in Ptolemaic Egypt, in debts incurred between private individuals.   Paragraph 7 deals with cases of complete default of the debtors, the result being sale into outright slavery.   It is the ὑπόχρεον σῶμα of paragraph 6 who calls for particular attention.   What was his status and what were the processes which led to that status?   In so far as the official attitude and the fiscal department were concerned the condition was one of slavery, just as the debtor slave (ὁ κατακείμενος) of the Gortyn law was a slave in the eyes of the lawmaker.   The reduction to the status of ὑπόχρεα σώματα occurred by the following steps.   Being free persons, they had borrowed money upon the security of their property and ultimately of their persons.   There is a strong probability that execution on the person would only be taken in case their property did not suffice, at the termination of the period of the loan, to meet the obligation incurred.[158] While still free (ἐλεύθερα ὄντα) they had voluntarily (ἑαυ[τά]) taken some step (the verb is missing) which would lead to the satisfaction of the claims of the creditor.   It was this action which changed the status of the debtors from that of free persons to that of debtor slaves.   The state, thereupon, collected a slave sale tax, distributed in equal parts upon the debtor and the

[156] P. Halensis 1, lines 219-221.

[157] See the discussion, *Dikaiomata*, pp. 122-124: ὁ Ἀλεξανδρεὺς τῶι Ἀλεξα[ν]δρεῖ μὴ δουλέτω μηδὲ ἡ Ἀλεξανδρὶς τῶι Ἀλεξα[ν]δρεῖ μηδὲ τῆι Ἀλ[ε]ξανδρίδι.

[158] This is suggested by analogy with the penal action in the city laws of Alexandria: πραξάτω ὁ πράκτωρ ἢ ὁ ὑπηρετὴς ἐκ τῶν ὑπαρχόντων καθάπερ ἐκ δίκη[ς, ἐὰν δὲ μὴ ἐκποιῆι καὶ ἐκ τοῦ] σώματος, P. Hal. 1, 119-120.

creditor. It is an important factor in the situation that the tax was taken upon the creation of the slave status of the debtor, not upon its cessation. The debtor was regarded as the equivalent of the seller of the slave in the customary transfers of slaves in paragraph 1, as one who had disposed of his own personal services, the creditor as the purchaser of the slave.

Combining the new information upon the debtor slaves in P. Col. Inv. 480 and that concerning execution upon the person for torts in P. Hal. 1, 117-120 with the knowledge gained from P. Hal. I 219-221 that even a citizen of Alexandria might be sold into slavery, one further deduction regarding the ὑπόχρεα σώματα is warranted. Two possibilities existed for the debtor who had guaranteed payment with his property and his person, but could not satisfy his obligation with his property. He might voluntarily submit himself to the debtor as an ὑπόχρεον σῶμα (self-submission to bondage, P. Col. Inv. 480, paragraph 6),[159] or he might be sold into slavery (paragraph 7). Whether this was a matter of option on the part of the debtor, or determined by decision of the creditor; whether sale into slavery could only follow after the debtor has had, as ὑπόχρεον σῶμα, an opportunity to repay his debt and has failed in his attempt[160]—these are questions to which the evidence does not afford an answer. P. Hal. 1, 219-221 has proven that citizens of Alexandria could be sold into slavery for debt, with the restrictions already discussed. It is unthinkable that the milder measure, of entrance into the status of debtor bondage, accepted in the Greek law of the sixth century, would be denied to them, seeing that P. Col. Inv. 480 indicates that debtor bondage was a measure applicable to all Egyptian subjects about 200 B.C. In that case we have the further information, important to the problem of the ὑπόχρεα σώματα, that entrance into debtor bondage was a general possibility open to

[159] Legalists have long insisted that self-mancipation of a free man by direct execution was unknown to Roman law: Savigny, *Vermischte Schriften* I, Berlin, 1850, p. 399. The right of self-sale or self-pledge by contract has, however, been well established. See Zulueta, *Law Quarterly Review* XXIX (1913), p. 150. The latter action is what occurs in the case of the ὑπόχρεα σώματα in P. Col. Inv. 480. Self-submission of free men into slavery for debt seems to have been known in Egypt in the sixth century B.C. See Griffith, *Dem. Pap. in the Rylands Lib.* III p. 51.

[160] This latter conclusion is suggested as the correct one by the analogy of the defeated accuser in cases of bodily assault in P. Hal. 1, 117-121. In such cases execution was compulsory upon the property if it sufficed to meet the recompense imposed upon the accuser. Only in case the property of the accuser did not suffice could execution upon his person follow.

the free population of Egypt, both Greeks and natives, except where special considerations of government policy might exempt certain classes. An exemption from magisterial execution upon the person appears in the amnesty decree of Euergetes II, of 118 B.C., affecting the royal peasants, those engaged in the government service of tax collection, and others not specified (P. Teb. 5). These are economically essential classes. Being exempt from bodily execution by the *praktores xenikon*, they must also, as representing essential services, have been precluded from self-submission to slavery for debt. This was not explicitly stated in the decree of Euergetes II, but would be implicit, as a milder measure against debtors, in the exemption from magisterial execution.

In discussing the means of agricultural production Varro states that fields are cultivated by human labor, which may be that of slaves, or of free men, or of both classes. He enumerates three kinds of free labor—poor peasant owners, hired hands, and "those whom our people call debtors (*obaerarii*)—and even now they exist in Asia and in Egypt and in Illyricum, many of them."[161] I follow the conviction of Hans Lewald upon the *obaerarii* of Varro, that this type of field labor had formerly existed in the Roman Republic[162] and that they were bonded debtors.[163] It is true that Varro includes them among his types of free labor. But this is probably a jurist's decision as to status, based upon the observation of the limited term of their bondage. In that case it follows that the *obaerarii*, who still existed in Egypt in Varro's time, must be identified with the ὑπόχρεα σώματα of P. Col. Inv. 480. Varro's definition of the *nexus* goes back to one Mucius, commonly identified with the jurist, Quintus Mucius Scaevola. It describes him as a *free man* who had given his labor into servitude in return for money which he owed. He was called a *nexus* until he absolved his debt. The definition concludes with the remark, *ut ab aere obaeratus*.[164] The similarities of Varro's definition of the *nexi-obaerati*[165] with the condition of the ὑπόχρεα σώματα are striking.

---

[161] Varro, *Rerum Rusticarum* I 17, 12. For the criticism of the reading *idque* for *iique* in this passage in Varro, which would reduce Varro's three free types to two, see Lewald, *Zur Personalexekution*, pp. 7-9.

[162] Varro, *loc. cit.: iique quos obaerarios nostri vocitaverunt*.

[163] Lewald, *Zur Personalexekution*, p. 9.

[164] *De ling. Lat.* VII 105: *Liber qui suas operas in servitutem pro pecunia quam debet dat, dum solveret, nexus vocatur, ut ab aere obaeratus.* Though the passage is corrupt its general meaning is clear.

[165] For the identity of *nexi-obaerati* see Lewald, *Personalexekution*, p. 10, note 2.

A free man (*liber*, Varro; ἐλεύθερα ὄντα, P. Col. Inv. 480) had incurred debt (*pro pecunia quam debet*, Varro; ὑπόχρεα, P. Col. Inv. 480). He had transferred his personal services according to Varro (*suas operas . . . dat*); he had voluntarily taken some action in regard to the debt in P. Col. Inv. 480 (ἐαυ||[τὰ c. 10 letters]τὸ χρέος). Thereby, in Varro, his labor fell into bondage (*suas operas in servitutem . . . dat*); and he became technically a slave in P. Col. Inv. 480 (σῶμα, and the collection of the slave sale tax). It must be observed that, because of the purely fiscal character of the section of the *diagramma* here preserved, there is not the slightest indication in P. Col. Inv. 480 as to how the ὑπόχρεα σώματα might ultimately have satisfied their obligations to the creditor—whether by their personal services alone, as field laborers, house servants, or by use of such other technical or specialized faculties as they possessed; or whether only by paying the sum of the debt, their personal services being nevertheless bonded and perhaps regarded as due to the creditor in lieu of interest payments.[166] The further warning must be given that the correspondence of *nexi-obaerati*, the Egyptian *obaerarii*, and the ὑπόχρεα σώματα can only be regarded as one of close analogy, not one of identity.[167] The *nexum* was a Roman institution in origin and development. It applied to Roman citizens only. The ὑπόχρεον σῶμα status was Greco-Egyptian.[168] It applied, as has been shown, to all free subjects of the Ptolemies.

The analogy is close enough, however, to affect in one particular the controversy regarding the *nexum*.[169] In the case of the ὑπόχρεα σώματα of Ptolemaic Egypt it is apparent (P. Col. Inv. 480, 23-24) that entrance into the bondage status resulted in consequence of some act of self-mancipation on the part of the debtor, not as a result of the contract of debt itself. This gives the support, at least, of an analogy in ancient comparative law, to Mitteis' contention[170] that a second transaction occurred in the transfer from

[166] This same problem persists in the *nexus* controversy. See Ludwig Mitteis in *Sav.-Ztsch.* XXII p. 121.
[167] The distinction has been carefully maintained by Lewald in his excellent study, *Zur Personalexekution.*
[168] Pharaonic Egyptian precedent appears in the demotic documents of the sixth century already cited. Griffith, *Dem. Pap. in the Rylands Lib.* III 50-51.
[169] F. de Zulueta has an excellent summary of the opposing views on the *nexum* in *The Law Quarterly Review* XXIX (1913), pp. 137-153.
[170] *Sav.-Ztsch.* XXII pp. 118-125. Mitteis' view of *nexum inire, se nexum dare*, was adopted by Lewald, *Personalexekution*, pp. 11-12.

Roman citizen status to that of a *nexus*, by which the right of ownership of the debtor's person devolved upon the creditor. Whether this second transaction was the *nexum*, and the further consequences which may be drawn for the *nexus* problem, are matters for the jurists to decide, as indeed are other of the questions raised by the Columbia *diagramma*.

THE TRAFFIC IN SLAVES

There remains the historical obligation to evaluate the bearing of P. Col. Inv. 480 upon the accepted view as to the extent and character of slavery in Ptolemaic Egypt.[171] Upon the economic side the fundamental view generally current for slavery in Ptolemaic and Roman Egypt is that published by Ulrich Wilcken in 1899.[172] The general conclusion of Wilcken, based upon his study of the ostraka and the papyri then available, was that slave labor had little importance either in handicrafts and industry or in agriculture in that country, while under Greek and Roman control.[173] Slaves were used chiefly in household service among the Greeks in Egypt;[174] and concubinage with their masters gave especial importance to female slaves in these Greek households.[175] In his study of the Zenon papyri[176] Rostovtzeff has expressed a different view upon the importance of slavery and the use of slaves in Ptolemaic Egypt of the middle of the third century B.C. Rostovtzeff believed that there were numerous factories in Alexandria in the time of Philadelphus like the woolen factory run by Apollonius at Memphis, that these factories "were probably run on Greek models," and "that *large masses of slaves were employed by the factory owners.*"[177] This theory is in itself highly attractive, upon the assumption that Greek enterprise had penetrated Egypt and put a new spirit into the whole economic life of the country, introducing Greek

---

[171] I confine myself in this discussion to the question of slavery in Ptolemaic Egypt alone.

[172] *Gr. Ostraka*, pp. 681-704. For the same view, confirmed by the materials which had accumulated meantime, see his *Papyruskunde, Grundzüge*, I 1, p. 20 (published in 1912).

[173] *Gr. Ostraka* I pp. 695-697 (for industry); pp. 702 f. (for agricultural production). Cf. *Papyruskunde, Grundzüge* I 1, p. 27. For similar views see W. Schubart, *Einführung in die Papyruskunde* (1918), pp. 416 f., and more recently M. Modica, *La Civiltà dell'Egitto Greco-Romano* (Rome, 1924), pp. 2, 40.

[174] Household slavery particularly evident in Greek houses. Schubart, *Einführung*, p. 417; Wilcken, *Grundzüge*, p. 260 and, with more recent evidence, *Archiv* VI p. 449.

[175] Wilcken, *Ostraka*, p. 687.

[176] Rostovtzeff, *A Large Estate in Egypt*, Madison, 1922.

[177] *Op. cit.*, p. 135; cf. p. 180. See also Rostovtzeff's more recent statement in *Cambridge Ancient History* VII p. 135.

business ideas, including the use of slaves in handicraft industry. Without question Greek organizing ability as applied in Egypt altered fundamentally the static economic system inherited from the Pharaohs. This new Greek spirit was perhaps at its zenith in the period of Philadelphus and particularly under the energetic leadership of Apollonius as Finance Minister. With these general assumptions those who have read the Zenon documents will no doubt be in complete accord.[178] At first sight the evidence of P. Col. Inv. 480, with its tax and fees on slave sales and its intricate regulations and organization for the collection of the tax, would seem to lend support to Rostovtzeff's view, and to imply that the numbers of the slaves in Ptolemaic Egypt have been too greatly minimized, and consequently that their importance in the life of the time has been underestimated. The decision as to the correctness of this conclusion must rest, in part, upon the validity of Rostovtzeff's claim, contrary to Wilcken's findings, of the use of many slaves in industrial work in Egypt under the earlier Ptolemies.

His view regarding the use of slaves in industry rests chiefly upon the appearance of the word $\pi\alpha\iota\delta\iota\sigma\kappa\eta$ in four of the Zenon papyri, P. Cairo Zenon III 59335, 48 (= P. Cairo Edgar 65);[179] P.S.I. VI 667; P.S.I. IV 371; and P. Lond. Inv. 2313.[180] In P. Cairo Zenon 59355 the context makes it clear that the $\pi\alpha\iota\delta\iota\sigma\kappa\eta$ is a slave girl; but we have no knowledge of the business in which the two slave girls of Philon, who appear in this papyrus, were used. If Philon is to be identified with the baker of Apollonius the dioecetes,[181] obviously he did not manage a bakery of his own. He was merely the personal baker of Apollonius, who accompanied him in his travels up and down the Nile. The slave girls used by him in the bakery were engaged in household service, not in industry.[182] The $\pi\alpha\iota\delta\iota\sigma\kappa\eta$ of P.S.I. 667 was a free girl, who carried wood (possibly engaged also in fishing). That she was free is

[178] See "The Greek Exploitation of Egypt," in *Political Science Quarterly* XL (1925), pp. 525-530, 538.

[179] Published by C. C. Edgar in *Annales du Service des Antiquités de l'Égypte* XXI (1921), pp. 89-108 and now republished as P. Cairo Zenon III 59355 (*Catalogue Général des Antiquités du Musée du Caire*, 1928).

[180] See Rostovtzeff, *Large Estate*, pp. 180, 65, 117, and 177 for citation of these documents in the order given above.

[181] See P. Cornell 1. 11 *et passim*, and 81-83 note.

[182] P. Cornell 1 198 note, with the possibility of identification of the slave girl who appears there with one of the two $\pi\alpha\iota\delta\iota\sigma\kappa\alpha\iota$ of Philon in P. Cairo Zenon III 59355.

proven by the fact that she expresses herself as unwilling to withdraw from the service of Zenon, as the rest of the girls did when they were treated unjustly.[183]   The loom-worker, Choirine, of P.S.I. 371 was quite clearly a free paid hand in the management of the Philadelphia estate.   She appears in an unpublished Columbia papyrus in a list of monthly salary payments in kind (wheat), along with a group of free men well known in Apollonius' organization.   Several of these—Ballion, Eutychus, and Numenius—appear in a similar list of monthly salary payments in money, including a money allowance for clothing (ἱματισμός), in another unpublished Columbia papyrus.[184] By this analysis the proof behind Rostovtzeff's statement regarding slave girls in *industry* is eliminated.   There remains only P. Lond. Inv. 2313 which has to do with slaves used in agriculture.   This document is not available to me.[185]   As in the case of παιδάριον and σῶμα, the translation "slave girl" may be given to παιδίσκη only where the context makes such meaning quite evident.   In P. Cairo Zenon III 59355, 48, τι[μὴ]ν π[αιδίσκης (cf. the related document 59356, lines 11-12), and in III 59374 it is evident that a slave girl is meant.   The use of π[α]ιδίσκην δ[ο]ύλην in P. Pet. I 12, 11[186] (cf. the correction in P. Pet. III 9. p. 18) shows that παιδίσκη alone is not decisive as to whether the status of the girl is free or slave.

A Zenon papyrus recently published by Edgar (P. Cairo Zenon III 59378) is a letter from a farm manager named Alcimus to Zenon urgently requesting that Zenon send back to him some slaves (παιδάρια) who were, in this case, working as farm hands.   "For," says Alcimus, "it is not fitting that I should bring in hired hands, and Theon should work without wages to pay."   It seems necessary to conclude, from the fact that the slaves had been transferred from Alcimus to Theon and must be returned to Alcimus if he were not to be compelled to use hired hands, that agricultural slaves were not

---

[183] οὐ θέλουσα ἀναχωρῆσαι [ἀπό] σου, P.S.I. 667, 3-4. ἀναχωρεῖν cannot here mean "run away."

[184] P. Col. Inv. 249.

[185] Rostovtzeff, *Large Estate*, p. 177, also uses P. Lond. Inv. 2312 to show the probable use of slave labor, accepting παιδάρια in this sense. But παιδάρια, like σώματα, cannot be so taken unless the references to slaves are clear. They are boys, free or slave, as the case may be.

[186] Period of Philadelphus, cf. U.P.Z. I 1 (late fourth century B.C.), where παιδίσκη means "girl," and Vitelli's note to P.S.I. VII 854, 19. In P. Cairo Zenon II 59142 the girl weavers may be either free or slave or both. Edgar takes them to be slave girls.

numerous, even upon the gift estate of the great and powerful Apollonius. At best the use of slaves in farm work evidenced in this document is quite untypical of the conditions prevailing in the Zenon correspondence. The position taken by Wilcken, and generally followed since the appearance of his *Griechische Ostraka*, remains unshaken by the more recent evidence, even for the reign of Philadelphus as evidenced in the Zenon papyri. Allowance should be made for the appearance of large numbers of slaves in the Egyptian market at certain times during the third century B.C. because of successful foreign wars. An example of this probably lies before us in P. Gradenwitz 1, as explained by Wilcken. Although P. Col. Inv. 480 gives no indication of the uses to which slaves were put, it gives support to the older view that the slave traffic was relatively unimportant in the economic life of Ptolemaic Egypt. It may be necessary to make an exception for Alexandria, as Rostovtzeff has recently indicated in *Cambridge Ancient History* VII 135. But even for Alexandria what little information we have would indicate that the freedmen who played so important a part in Egyptian life in the time of Augustus (according to Strabo 797) were personages of considerable importance and that they did not rise from the ranks of slave handicraftsmen. The women slaves who appear in Alexandria in papyri of the Augustan period were chiefly rented out by their owners as nurses, or were entrusted with the rearing of slave children. Therefore the work which they did, even in Alexandria, seems to have been work connected with the household, not with the handicrafts.[187]

Though the sales of slaves in paragraph 1 of P. Col. Inv. 480 were by private contract and slave-selling was not a government monopoly,[188] the previous discussion has shown how closely the Ptolemaic government regulated such sales. We have, unfortunately, only a small section of the *diagramma* on the slaves. How far its regulations went can not be determined. But the government required the declaration of all slaves offered for sale. It controlled, through its officials, the auctioning system, even in the sales between private

---

[187] Wilhelm Schubart, *Archiv für Papyrusforschung* V pp. 116-118.

[188] Compare the purchase of slaves in the open market in Idumaea for Zenon (P. Cairo Zenon 59015, *verso*); the slave purchase, probably at Gaza, by Menecles of Tyre for shipment from Tyre to Egypt (P. Cairo Zenon 59093); the ὠνὴ παιδίσκης from Nicanor to Zenon (P. Cairo Zenon I 59003); P.S.I. IV 406; and B.G.U. VI 1259, of 100/99 B.C.

individuals (P. Col. Inv. 480, paragraphs 1-3). The remarkably high tax on sales (ranging around twenty per cent *ad valorem*) might *per se* be regarded as a check upon slave transfers, particularly when compared with the Roman four per cent tax on slave sales.[189] A twenty per cent tax on transfers would certainly tend to limit home breeding of slaves for sale. Slave-breeding for the market does not seem to have been a marked characteristic of Ptolemaic Egypt; and the law forbidding export of slaves would certainly operate strongly against it.[190] When the high tax upon slave sales is combined with an import duty upon slaves exacted in the parts of Syria under Egyptian control, the tendency toward restriction of the traffic becomes very marked.[191] Neither in P. Col. Inv. 480, nor in P. Grad. 1, nor in P. Hibeh 29 does any trace of professional slave dealers appear.[192] This fact, also, is significant.

The question arises whether the indications of a Ptolemaic policy against encouragement of the slave traffic, cited above, may have been carried to the extent of active discouragement of the practice, expressed in legislation to that end. There is no proof of such legislation, unless it may be seen in the requirement that a special permit was needed for the export of slaves from Syrian harbors under control of the Egyptian government. This permit was called an ἐξαγωγή, and it was *not* required for ordinary goods.[193] One is certainly justified in saying that the situation created by the government's regulatory provisions was such as to limit the traffic greatly. Such a policy was advisable in a country in which the density of population was relatively high and a cheap form of effective free labor was already at hand in the native Egyptian population. Particularly in the situation created by the stirrings of the Egyptian native spirit after the battle of Raphia in 217 B.C., any encouragement of competition of slave labor against the native free labor, either

---

[189] Tacitus, *Annals*, XIII 31.

[190] P. Lille 29, I 13, of the third century B.C. (= Mitteis, *Chrest.* 369; =Meyer, *Jur. Papyri*, 71), μηθενὶ ἐξέστω σώματα πωλεῖν [ἐπ'] ἐξαγωγῆι. The law against export certainly denotes a strong regulating interest in slavery on the part of the government, but its operation would be restrictive. For a contrary view see Rostovtzeff in *C.A.H.* VII 135.

[191] Proven by P. Cairo Zenon 59093. I cannot agree with Rostovtzeff, *Large Estate*, p. 34, that the import of slaves from Syria into Egypt was not permitted. P. Cairo Zenon I 59093 proves the contrary.

[192] In fact, slave dealers (σωματέμποροι) are attested for Greco-Roman Egypt only in the sixth Christian century, so far as my knowledge goes. See P. Strass. Inv. 1404, 24, 127, edited by Preisigke in *Archiv* III pp. 415 ff.

[193] P. Cairo Zenon I 59093, 10-13.

in industry or in agriculture, would have been folly for the paternalistic-absolutistic dynasty of the Ptolemies. It was, after all, a foreign dynasty, become national by virtue of political necessity; and as a foreign dynasty it was peculiarly subject to the pressure of the native feeling.

Against these arguments stands the impression left by the regulations of P. Col. Inv. 480 that a considerable amount of slave-selling went on. The *dorea* of Dicaearchus consisted, in its later form, only of the clerical fee upon forced sales by the government (paragraphs 4-5), with the possible additions of the clerical fees on transfers of free men to the status of debtor bondage and on sales for debt (paragraphs 6-7). It is a fair assumption that his income from this source must have been large. If we imagine, in the complete lack of evidence, sales of slaves amounting to ten thousand in the year and that only one thousand of these were brought about by fiscal delinquencies and hence assignable to Dicaearchus, we have an annual *dorea* coming in to him of ten minas. This was in addition to his salary—one mina per day, if we may believe the statement of Polybius regarding the salaries paid to the captains under Scopas and assign to Dicaearchus the same salary as the other captains received.[194] The numbers given above are pure speculation. But they may help to illustrate two points. With a relatively small number of slave transfers in Egypt, such as would not appreciably affect labor conditions except in household work in the homes of the ruling Greek class, the government must nevertheless pass its regulations upon the traffic, surely for fiscal purposes, probably also for purposes of economic control of this form of labor supply. Furthermore, even though his clerical fee might be small, as coming from a limited number of transfers, the *dorea* of Dicaearchus would be acceptable as an extra emolument not required by any corresponding extra service upon his part. From the last point of view the *dorea* of Dicaearchus stands in complete contrast to the well-known *dorea* estate of the dioecetes Apollonius. The great farm of Apollonius and its development by irrigation laid a heavy burden upon the time, energy and resources of the man, in addition to his duties as Finance Minister.[195]

[194] Polybius XIII 3.

[195] Westermann, "Egyptian Agricultural Labor under Ptolemy Philadelphus," in *Agricultural History* I (1927), p. 47.

A summary of the new material upon slavery in Ptolemaic Egypt shows the following situation:[196]

Sources of slaves:[197]

a)   By foreign wars.[198]

b)   By purchase. The Zenon papyri indicate that Palestine and lower Syria were the chief sources of purchased slaves in the third century B.C.[199]

c)   By enslavement for debts to government and to private individuals.[200]

d)   By slave birth in homes of masters—probably greatly limited by reason of concubinage.

Prices of slaves. Several exact prices are now known from the Zenon papyri for slave purchases in the middle of the third century B.C. In a list of receipts and expenditures of an agent who visited Sidon and Ascalon there is an expenditure of 112 drachmas for a $\pi\alpha\hat{\iota}s$,[201] which must be for a slave purchase. In 259 B.C. Zenon bought a young girl, named Sphragis, aged seven, for fifty drachmas.[202] A male slave was sold *in the Hauran* for 150 drachmas (no doubt he would have been rated higher in the market of Alexandria) and a girl slave was bought for 300 drachmas.[203] Zenon had received from Philon two slave women, mother and daughter, whose value was to be applied on a debt owed by Philon to Zenon. The two were evaluated, in application upon the debt, at their purchase price, namely 133 drachmas 2

---

[196] For a recent summary covering Greco-Roman Egypt in general, see Modica's *Civiltà dell'Egitto Greco-Romano*, pp. 147-151. The summary given by me makes no claim to be a complete study based upon an exhaustive search for all the material.

[197] Cf. Modica, *La Civiltà*, p. 148.

[198] Implied in P. Grad. 1 and Ps.-Aristeas, par. 22. See Wilcken's letter in *Sitz. Heid. Akad., phil.-hist. Kl.* V (1914), 15 Abh. Slaves from Punt were rare according to Wilcken in *Ztsch. für Aegypt. Sprache* LX (1925), p. 101.

[199] P. Cairo Zenon I 59010 ($\tau o\hat{\upsilon}$ $\pi\alpha\iota\delta\acute{o}s$, line 26), 59015 *verso*, 59076, 59077; P.S.I. IV 406; Wilcken in *Archiv* VI p. 449; and cf. the Syrian slave in U.P.Z. 121, of 156 B.C. See also L. H. Vincent, "La Palestine dans les Papyrus Ptolemaiques," in *Rev. Bibl.*, 1920, pp. 161-202; George McLean Harper, Jr., "Study in the Commercial Relations between Egypt and Syria," in *A.J.P.* XLIX (1928) pp. 1-35.

[200] P. Col. Inv. 480, 15-29. For execution, in private loans, $\pi\rho\hat{\alpha}\xi\iota s$ $\dot{\epsilon}\kappa$ $\tau o\hat{\upsilon}$ $\delta\epsilon\delta\alpha\nu\epsilon\iota\sigma\mu\acute{\epsilon}\nu o\upsilon$ $\kappa\alpha\grave{\iota}$ $\tau\hat{\omega}\nu$ $\dot{\upsilon}\pi\alpha\rho\chi\acute{o}\nu\tau\omega\nu$ $\alpha\dot{\upsilon}\tauo\hat{\upsilon}$ $\pi\acute{\alpha}\nu\tau\omega\nu$ $\kappa\alpha\theta\acute{\alpha}\pi\epsilon\rho$ $\dot{\epsilon}\kappa$ $\delta\acute{\iota}\kappa\eta s$, see L. Mitteis, *Reichsrecht und Volksrecht*, pp. 401 ff.; Angelo Segrè, in *Aegyptus* VIII (1927) pp. 325-331.

[201] P. Cairo Zenon I 59010, 26.

[202] P. Cairo Zenon I 59003, 5.

[203] P.S.I. IV 406, 17-19, 25-26.

obols, or 66 2/3 drachmas each.[204] The range of the known prices is, therefore, for a girl, from 50 drachmas to 300 drachmas, for a male slave from 112 drachmas to 150 drachmas (for one sold in the Hauran). To this we may add the observation that in P. Grad. 1 the range of prices suggested for a sale, which was apparently of a special kind, was 1, 2 and 3 minas. That the prices of male slaves in the third century ran well over a mina is also suggested by letters of Zenon, drafted in the year 259 or 258 B.C. in Alexandria regarding three runaway slaves.[205] Zenon gave orders to pay to informers,[206] who had reported where the slaves were to be found, the reward which the informers demanded, namely, 100 drachmas, or 33 1/3 drachmas for each slave.

The taxes collected upon slaves, as far as the evidence at present indicates, did not include an ownership tax. They were as follows:

(1) An import duty, with necessity of a special permit for importing from harbors under Egyptian control.[207]

(2 Taxes and fees on sales, whether arranged between private individuals or under direct conduct of the government.

(3) Tax and fees upon transfers of free men into debtor bondage, as *hypochrea somata*, and upon ultimate sale of such persons.[208]

(4) Tax on emancipations and manumissions of slaves. The tax on emancipations of slaves appears in P. Hibeh 29, 6-7. A mortgaged slave who has informed upon an owner who has attempted to escape the sale tax is to be freed; but the emancipated slave must pay the customary tax on emancipations. The editors, in the note to line 7, have pointed out that these can not be the regular sale taxes, for which the slave owner would remain responsible. The emancipation tax was, in this instance, taken from the slave who had been freed. Though no Ptolemaic example of a manumission tax is known to me, I assume that such a tax was exacted. It existed in many of the

[204] P. Cairo Edgar in *Annales du Service* XXI 65 (= P. Cairo Zenon III 59355) 48-53, 68-70.

[205] P. Cairo Zenon I 59015 *verso*. In P.S.I. IV 424 a man proposes to pledge his son to Zenon at 100 drachmas. It is, in my judgment, a case of pledging for debt, not one of apprenticing the boy for a public career, as the editor suggests. Note line 13, ὑποθέσιν σοι αὐτόν, and cf. ὁ ὑποτεθείς of P. Hibeh 29 *recto*.

[206] Understanding, with Wilcken (U.P.Z. I, p. 569-570), that the informers (μηνυτρίζοντες) are the same as οἱ αἰτοῦντες, namely, those demanding the reward.

[207] P. Cairo Zenon I 59093, 10-13.

[208] P. Col. Inv. 480, 23-29.

contemporary Hellenistic city-states,[209] and is found later in Egypt under Roman control.[210]   The amount and incidence of the manumission tax may have been included in the lost portion of P. Col. Inv. 480 in col. II.[211]

Upon the delicts of slaves, degree of obligation of owners when innocent of participation or party to the crime, we have a very important Ptolemaic document of the third century.   For the information which it has brought, see the references cited below,[212] especially that to Paul M. Meyer's *Juristische Papyri*.

In connection with the traffic in slaves with the dealers in Syria and for identification purposes in other sales, the purchaser was furnished a complete description of the particular slave or slaves transferred.   We have such descriptions in the case of four boy slaves sent by Tobiah (Greek, Toubias), the Ammonite *sheik*, to Apollonius.[213]   The description may include name, age, coloring (complexion and eyes), peculiarities of shape of face, hair (if curly), scars or wens, whether circumcised or uncircumcised,[214] or other physical features such as stature, bearded or beardless, tatooing, dress.[215]   In the case of runaway slaves, notices were posted with offer of reward for information leading to apprehension and return of the slave.   In P. Paris 10, the one clear example which we have from Ptolemaic Egypt, the notice was an official one.[216]   In the case of the three runaway slaves of Zenon the amount of the reward was fixed by demand of the men who claimed it, with agreement thereto by Zenon.   Customarily, however, the amount of the reward was fixed by the masters of the slaves.[217]

[209] A. Calderini, *La manomissione e la condizione dei liberti in Graecia*, Milan, 1908, 136-142.

[210] P. Freib. 10 (*Sitz. Heid. Akad.* VII), republished by P. M. Meyer, *Jur. Papyri*, 7, line 6, with references.

[211] For the legal consequences of manumission in Egypt in the Roman period, see Modica, *La civiltà*, p. 150.

[212] P. Lille 29.   See Mitteis, *Chrest.* 369, and Meyer, *Jur. Papyri*, 71, with full references to the literature upon the document.

[213] P. Cairo Zenon I 59076.

[214] So in P. Cairo Zenon I 59076.

[215] As in P. Par. 10 (=U.P.Z. 121).

[216] Wilcken, U.P.Z. I, p. 568.

[217] See Wilcken's acute discussion of P. Par. 10 in his introduction to U.P.Z. 121.   See the same discussion for right of asylum of slaves, and cf. Fr. von Woess, *Das Asylwesen Aegyptens in der Ptolemäerzeit*, Munich, 1923, pp. 175-179.

INDICES

INDEX OF PASSAGES CITED

65

GREEK WORDS APPEARING IN P. COL. INV. 480 AND
FRAGMENT OF INV. 228

ἀγοράζειν: 3 ll. 8, 11, 16, 20

ἀγορανόμος: 3 l. 4

ἀνδράποδον: 3 ll. 1, 2, 8

ἀνθυπερβολή: 3 l. 13

ἀντιγραφεύς: 3 l. 3

ἀπογράφειν: 4 l. 30; 28 l. 2

ἀποδιδόναι: 3 ll. 6, 10

ἀργύριον: 3 l. 5

αὐθήμερον: 4 l. 30

βασιλικός (πρὸς βασιλικά): 3 l. 19

γραφῖον: 3 l. 18; 4 ll. 21, 26, 29

δανείζειν: 4 ll. 24, 25

διάγραμμα: 3 l. 3

Δικαίαρχος: 3 l. 7; 4 l. 21

δωρεά: 3 ll. 7, 17; 4 l. 22; 28 l. 1

ἑαυτός: 4 l. 23

ἑκατοστή: 3 ll. 16, 17; 4 ll. 21, 28

ἐλεύθερος: 4 l. 23

ἔχειν: 28 l. 1

καταβάλλειν: 3 l. 11

καταγράφειν: 3 ll. 4, 5

κατέχειν: 3 l. 13

κηρύκειον: 3 ll. 17, 20

λογεύειν: 3 l. 7

μνᾶ: 3 ll. 8, 9, 12, 16, 20; 4 ll. 25, 26; 28 l. 2

πόλις: 3 ll. 9, 12, 14

πραγματεύειν (ὁ πραγματευόμενος): 3 l. 2

πράκτωρ ξενικῶν: 3 l. 15

πράττειν: 3 ll. 3, 12, 16, 19; 4 ll. 24, 27

προπρατικόν: 3 l. 14

προπωλητικόν: 3 l. 9

προσκαταβάλλειν: 3 l. 14

πωλεῖν: 3 ll. 15, 19

σῶμα: 3 ll. 3, 10, 12, 18; 4 ll. 22, 23, 26, 29

τέλος: 3 l. 11

τιμή: 3 l. 5

ὑπερβολή: 3 l. 13

ὑπόχρεος: 4 l. 23

χρέος: 4 ll. 24, 27

ὠνή: 3 ll. 2, 4

SUBJECT INDEX

COLUMBIA UNIVERSITY PRESS
COLUMBIA UNIVERSITY
NEW YORK

———

FOREIGN AGENT
OXFORD UNIVERSITY PRESS
HUMPHREY MILFORD
AMEN HOUSE, LONDON, E.C.

Bei Fragen zur Produktsicherheit wenden Sie sich bitte an:
If you have any questions regarding product safety,
please contact:

Walter de Gruyter GmbH
Genthiner Straße 13
10785 Berlin
productsafety@degruyterbrill.com